ONE GOLDEN NUGGET

Business Blunders
and Bloody Great Ideas

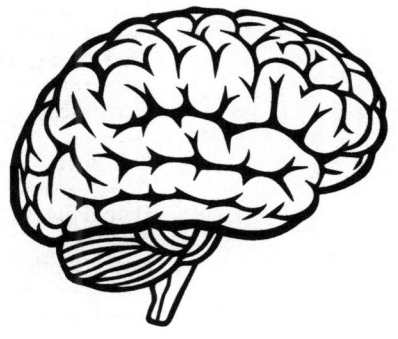

John Attridge C.T.B.

Nugget Contributors

Below are all the people who contributed their Nuggets of wisdom to this book. Thank you!

Alison Edgar MBE *Customer 4 years*	45	David Cliff *Customer 6 years*	130
Alistair Greener *Mutual thought leader*	92	David Harding *Client 19 years*	130
Andrew Bailey *Business Connection*	11	David Johnstone *Ex business partner(13yrs) Friend (38yrs)*	89
Andrew Banks *LinkedIn connection*	46	Dominic Ricciardi *Customer 7 years*	89
Andy Bounds *Quantum Leap workshop host*	46	Dr Jacqui Taylor *LinkedIn connection*	113
Andy Lennox *Business acquaintance 15 years*	9	Dr Phil Jauncey *Known for 46 years*	28
Andy Taylor – Whyte *Quantum Leap guest*	47	Dr Richard Strongman *Friend 15 years*	114
Angela De Souza *Customer event guest*	50	Ed Zia *Business connection 5 years*	113
Barbara Cox-Lovesy *Nutritional expert and author*	29	Frank King *Quantum Leap guest*	108
Barry Cusack *Friend of 40 years*	48	Fred Dinage MBE *Interviewed Quantum Leap*	13
Bernie Davies *Quantum Leap guest*	73	Geoff Head *Friend*	133
Blanche van Berckel *Linked in connection*	9	Gill Bevis *Personal contact 15 years*	47
Bob Meyer *Industry connection of 31 years*	74	Hatty Fawcett *Friend*	108
Brian Esposito *Linked in connection*	73	Holly Smith *Quantum Leap guest*	12
Chanelle McCoy *LinkedIn connection*	72	Ivor Tucker *Association contact*	112
Chong Kee Tan *IRTA associate*	75	Jacqui Frampton *Customer and connection 10 years*	10
Chuck Reeves *Interviewed Quantum Leap*	28	James Short CB OBE *Quantum Leap guest*	114
Claire Byrne *Linked In connection*	27	James Sinclair *Customer*	139
Craig Duffy *Sporting contact 30 years*	72	Janet Kelly *Customer*	69
Croz Crossley *Friend 5 years*	131	Jarvis Smith *LinkedIn connection*	138
Darryl Bannon *Friend and fellow podcaster*	92	Jeff Fenech *Interviewed Quantum Leap*	12
David Brock *Customer 15 years*	132	Joe Foster *Quantum Leap guest*	44

Joe Pici *Quantum Leap guest*	45	Michael Chittenden *Client for 15 years*	87
John Parrett *Client 20 years*	45	Michael Trigg *Personal contact 11 years*	71
John Shenton *Customer and supplier 6 years*	139	Mike Perry *Customer colleague and friend 15 years*	94
John Treharne *LinkedIn contact*	111	Monty Munford *LinkedIn connection*	8
John Tschohl *Customer 17 years*	136	Nigel Apperley *Client 5 years*	90
Jon Dutton *Interviewed on Quantum Leap*	115	Paul Bohill *Quantum Leap guest*	26
Josh Simons *Known 15 years*	137	Paul Hargreaves *Associate 5 years*	107
Jules White *Business connection 4 years*	138	Penny Power OBE *Business associate*	86
Kath Pay *Connection 20 years*	133	Priya Mishr *Networking connection*	109
Keith Abraham *Linked In connection*	30	Professor Allan Pease *Known for 40 years*	13
Kevin Byrne *Interviewed Quantum Lea*	70	Richard Flint *LinkedIn connection*	87
Kim Strabley *Fellow IRTA member*	111	Rick Powell *Friend and business colleague*	69
Lance Scouler *Customer*	135	Rick Terrien *LinkedIn connection*	109
Les Abbott – Fryer *Customer on and off 15 years*	135	Robert Jones *LinkedIn connection*	107
Liz Brewer *Quantum Leap guest*	106	Ron Whitney *Industry connection 20 years*	26
Lizzie McManus *Customer*	67	Sally Marshall *Customer Quantum Leap workshop host*	106
Lord Mark Price *Quantum Leap guest*	110	Scott Fitzpatrick *Quantum Leap guest*	91
Maddy Alexander Grout *Customer*	134	Scott Parazynski *Business connection*	90
Malcolm Larri *Linked in connection and Quantum Leap events*	94	Scott Whitmer *Friend and IRTA colleague 32 years*	91
Marc Ferguson *LinkedIn connection*	93	Steve Bicknell *Client 20 years*	67
Martin Tindall *Business contact 22 years*	88	Steve Jones *Client for 15 years*	50
Mary Pagano *Linked in connection*	132	Steve Legg *Customer 12 years*	48
Mel Fisher *Chief Opportunity Advisor Business For Breakfast*	88	Steve McKenna *Networking connection*	68
Melissa Smith *Quantum Leap guest*	10	Steve Williams *Friend 41 years*	49

Susan Gruenwald 66
Competitor known 30 years
Tim Bishop 51
Client 20 years
Tom Ball 51
LinkedIn Connection
Tom Greco 65
Association connection 30 years
Tony Brown 29
Customer and acquaintance 12 years
Tony Robinson OBE 64
LinkedIn contact
Tracey Smolinski 30
Customer 5 years
Trevor Nel 31
Networking and Quantum Leap
Unisa Kamara 49
LinkedIn contact
Warren Ostergard 31
Competitor
Will Bellow 64
Customer 4 years
William Sachiti 66
LinkedIn connection

This edition first published 2021
© 2021

Registered office
7-8 Church Street, Wimborne, Dorset, BH21 1JH, United Kingdom

For details of our global editorial office, for customer services and for information about how to apply for permission to reuse the copyright material in this book please see our website at www.onegoldennugget.com

The right of the author to be identified as the author of this work has been asserted in accordance with the Copyright, Designs and Patents Act 1988.

All rights reserved. No part of this publication may be reproduced, stored in a retrival system, or transmitted, in any form or by any means, electronic, mechanical, photocopying, recording or otherwise, except as permitted by the UK Copyright, Designs and Patents Act 1988, without the prior permission of the publisher.

One Golden Nugget also publishes its books in a variety of electronic formats. Some content that appears in print may not be available in electronic books.

Designations used by companies to distinguish their products are often claimed as trademarks. All brand names and product names used in this book are trade names, service marks, trademarks or registered trademarks of their respective owners. The publisher is not associated with any product or vendor mentioned in this book. This publication is designed to provide acurate and authoritative information in regard to the subject matter covered.
It is sold on the understanding that the publisher is not engaged in rendering professional services. If professional advice or other expert assistance is required, the services of a competant professional should be sort.

Cover & Book Design
David Torres Mora

Published by One Golden Nugget

Dedication

To those that I have in some way come in contact with over the four decades I have personally observed some blunders that by outlining but not naming personally in this book I hope to use as a beacon for the 100 million to not keep making the same ones!

For those looking for bloody great ideas - nothing is proprietary in business - you may have a trade mark or a patent - but ideas are simply a catalyst to be developed giving first to market sometimes an edge but not always - in fact therein lies the irony - often the second to market becomes the dominant player having benefited by hindsight.

Contents

Introduction	I
Chapter 1 - Let the journey begin	1
Pivotal Moment	14
Johnisms 1, 2 and 3	15
Chapter 2 - Expect the unexpected	19
Johnisms 4, 5 and 6	33
Chapter 3 - Launching BBX	37
Johnisms 7, 8 and 9	53
Chapter 4 - Growing BBX	57
Johnisms 10, 11 and 12	77
Chapter 5 - Growth can kill you!	81
Johnisms 13, 14 and 15	97
Chapter 6 - Learn from history	101
Johnisms 16, 17 and 18	117
Pivotal Moment	120

Chapter 7 - Seek out solutions 123

Johnisms 19, 20, 21 and 22 143
John's case studies & random thoughts 147
Case Study One 148
Case Study Two 150
Case Study Three 151
AND ANOTHER THING… 152
AND ONE MORE THING… 153
Case Study Four - The Cat Café 155
Case Study Five - AFC Bournemouth 156
Case Study Six - Dealing with Crisis 158
Case Study Seven - Unsold capacity 161
Case Study Eight - Property 163
My Nuggets on recruitment 165

Gratitude 168

Introduction

My name is John Attridge and I have been in the digital trade credit space since 1989 and I'm CEO and founder of BBXUK. I founded the company in 2014 having assisted the BBX brand at home in Australia since it's formation in 1993 and we now operate in thirteen countries with more than 97,000 cardholders and 250 staff, it is the largest business community of its kind in the world. Essentially, we're an exchange network – we provide our business customers a way of trading with each other without the need to use conventional cash money.

It's pretty successful and I'm really grateful for that, but life hasn't always gone to plan which is why what you holding in your hands – my first book – Business Blunders and Bloody Great Ideas.

The purpose of this book is to share experiences and learning from my journey. It's about the challenges I've overcome, the interesting people I've encountered over the years of being in business, and the success I've had which, I should add, has come as a result of many temporary failures.

I've created businesses, founded businesses, grown businesses and exited businesses worth 8 figures in trade sales as well as stock market flotations. I love business!

Every single thing that I've learnt over the course of my business life has been non-proprietary – I've never invented anything. But what I have done is picked up ideas and expanded on them, running with them in ways that create a unique experience that can be replicated and shared.

So, I'm all about collaboration. I'm all about connections. I'm all about scratching one another's backs to get a better result. The old definition of continuing to do what you've always done yet expecting the result to be different holds as true today as it has done at any other time. The only change is you will NOT get what you always got because the competition will have already innovated!

In this book I will share nuggets of wisdom with you from not only my journey, but also some of the great people I have been fortunate enough to connect with over the years.

I've also included some pivotal moments from my life. You could also call them Sliding Door moments if you happen to have seen that particular movie. They are things that happen during the course of a life that, in that moment, you don't know are going to change your life forever. They can have a profound impact, not just on yourself, but on many, many people – sometimes hundreds, maybe even thousands of people who, as a direct result of these moments, end up being affected by what, at the time, seems very innocuous circumstances. Look out for them in this book – perhaps they might remind you of some of your own pivotal moments.

Welcome to Business Blunders and Bloody Great Ideas!

John

Chapter 1
Let the journey begin

When I left university, I still hadn't the faintest idea as to what I was going to do. I'd completed a social science degree specialising in economics and accountancy, and yet I had no plan for what I was going to use that course for, and I'm sure that resonates with a lot of people.

There was no clear, defined path. I really envy people that said: 'I wanted to be a widget maker when I was eight years old and I saw this happen.' They had a clear direction on what they were going to do for the rest of their life, but that never happened to me.

The first job I had was with Coca-Cola. On my first morning I went down to the factory, and the guy said: 'Oh, we've got a job for you. I'll take you out the back. There's five acres of broken pallets, and your job is to cannibalise the broken ones and to make them into whole pallets.' As a farmer's son, I knew a little bit about how to fix things. So I set about mending all those pallets.

About three months later, I had finally finished. What was five acres of broken, twisted pallets was now about an acre and a half of brand-new pallets. I touched base with the guy. This would've been the first time I'd been into the factory in three months. And the guy was astounded that I'd completed it. He said: 'John, that's great work. I think I'm going to promote you now because we don't have any more pallets to mend. You're going to go onto the bottle washer.'

I was sat on this big, giant machine putting in 24 bottles of soiled and dirty Coca-Cola bottles, that went through a washer in rows of 24 at a time and came out clean, hopefully, and not broken.

I soon realised that after a university education, this was not for me. I went down to the local dole office and said to the guy down there: 'What jobs are there?'

He was a little guy, small built, glasses, pale, and very uninspiring. This was my job centre coach. After about 10 minutes, he said: 'There's no jobs.' I said: 'What do you mean there's no jobs?' He said: 'No. Absolutely nothing for your skill set. There's nothing suitable. You're better off going onto the dole.' I went: 'Oh, okay.'

I'm walking out the door, and I see a sign, which said: 'Wanted: MLC Life Insurance rep.' I took the sign off the board and took it back to him and said: 'Hey. What about this?' And he said: 'Oh, that's no good. That's commission only.' I said: 'What's that?' And he said: 'Well, you don't get a salary. You don't get any benefits. You need a job where you get 'x' amount of income coming in every day.' And I said" 'Okay, but what else have you got?' And he said: 'Nothing.' So, I said: 'Well, this is better than nothing, surely?'

I went and talked to the sales manager at the company, a guy called Ren Forte, lovely fellow. He said: 'Oh, you can communicate okay. You've got an education. Why don't you start? I've got a job starting Monday as a life insurance rep.' I said: 'Great, what do I do?' He said: 'Well, I'll meet you at a certain street in Churchill in Victoria, and I'll show you on-the-job training.'

On the first day, door-to-door I was collecting life insurance premiums, and monthly collector premiums. So, I knocked on Mrs Smith's door, and she said: 'Here's your $10.' He showed me how to put it in the little book, and write, '$10. New month's payment.' I said goodbye to Mrs Smith, 'See you next month.' And then, next, Mrs Jones is next door to that, and so on and so on.

We went round there, and we missed about 40% of the people on the first day. So, Ren showed me how to follow up. And then said: 'I've got an unexpected trip, and I've got to go up to Melbourne to a managers' meeting. Can you go back and see the people that we didn't catch up with yesterday?' I said: 'Yeah, sure.' He said: 'I'll see you on Friday.'

So, I knocked on the first door the second day, and the reason why Mrs Jones wasn't there yesterday was she'd just had a baby. She said: 'Oh, here's your $20' or whatever it was for the premiums for the month, and she said: 'Now, Mr Baxter who used to do the run before you, John, every time I have a new baby, I've got to sign up a new insurance plan.' I went: 'Oh, okay.' She said: 'It's either pink for girls or blue for boys.' I went: 'Okay. What have you had?' She said: 'I've had a girl.' So, I got the pink form out and filled it out and added the $10 a month to the payment, and now the child's education plan was taken care of.

This went on and, over the 40 calls, I ended up making three sales. And then, I turned up, having not much clue as to what I was doing, on Friday with these three new contracts, put them on Ren's desk, and he nearly had a heart attack. He said: 'Where did you get these from? I haven't even taught you the training yet.' I said: 'Oh. Well, this is how it's ... I've just ran into these people, and they told me that's what Mr Baxter did, so all I've done is follow that.' He laughed his head off.

He said: 'Do you realise how much commission you've made this week? It's nearly $1,000.' Now, my rate for the week collecting premiums was $104. So, after five months of doing this, I ended up being in the MLC Achievers' Club for the year, they held an Achievers' Dinner, based on my first five months' commissions that I'd earned from selling a range of insurance products.

My only regret was not seeking out the weedy guy at the dole office and showing him my commission statements which would have been 10-12 times his annual safe public sector salary!

At the age of 21 I became the youngest superintendent in MLC's history in charge of a team of guys.

A Nugget learned here is even in those early days, be aware of the natural gifts you have. For me, selling was clearly my forte (pardon the pun) and this was just a first taste of it.

After MLC, I moved to the Gold Coast and reconnected with a guy called David Johnston who I'd played football with when I was the captain-coach of a football team in Goulburn. He came to town as a player, and he'd begun a car rental business. His uncle's, Colin, and Alan were Australia's largest Mazda dealers.

As it often does, one thing lead to another and I got involved. We ended up buying a whole whack of brand-new Mazda cars. Here we were, late 20s/early 30s, and walked out with just a personal guarantee that wasn't worth anything, no contracts, with a million dollars worth of cars. This was back in the heady days of 16% interest and no questions asked by banks!

A Nugget here is: 'Ask for what you want in life, people might just say yes!'

So, we started Westrent Mazda Car Rentals on the Gold Coast, and then started operating out of Brisbane and the Sunshine Coast as well during World Expo in 1988.

If anybody recalls, back then, it was such a busy time where all the countries in the world come together in one space to advertise their destination to the rest of the world. For a ten-month period, the six months of the Expo and the two months either side, we made money faster than we could ever spend it. There were so many people coming in, we had fights in the queue if someone didn't bring their car back on time because other people were ready to jump in the car and race off to Expo. This was a huge business and I loved it.

My retired dad, who owned a dairy farm for many years and milked cows twice a day came up to the Gold Coast to see this operation and just shook his head. With the amount of money that we were making, he just said: 'You have just completely landed on your feet young man. I've had to work so hard for all my money, and you've just fallen into this where making money is just so easy.' And that's what I thought as well. We were in the right spot at the right time and making money became so simple.

Fast-forward 12 months, and in 1989 we had a national commercial pilot strike. Every commercial pilot in Australia stopped flying and so my company that was renting cars to people jumping off airplanes was finished, almost overnight. It went from a great business with more than 100% occupancy because of the overlap to almost zero in three weeks.

We still had all the overheads of running the business – the lease payment to Mazda, rent payment to the landlords and staff wages – all the fixed costs were still in place, but we had no revenue. What the hell were we going to do? The bubble had well and truly burst – we were going to go broke.

Business Blunders and Bloody Great Ideas

Let's share wisdom!

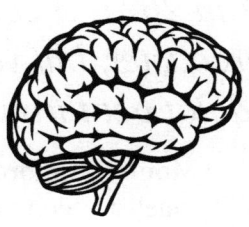

"I turned down a job in Amazon in 2000, at my old company in 2007 we were offered a 51% share in Angry Birds for $250K and turned it down, but persisted and finally hit gold at Sienna Network in 2021. A career has to be both fun and a rollercoaster, but you have to stay on the ride and not get thrown off, simple."

Monty Munford
Chief Evangelist - Sienna Network

*"There is no easy road, no right way,
there is just your way.
Listen, learn, be bold and be true to yourself.
Success takes time and its most certainly never easy."*

Andy Lennox
Founder, Restauranteur, Investor

*"Listen to advice of others, however
don't lose sight of your vision and
objective, mostly persevere and do not
give up, no matter what.'*

Blanche van Berckel
Founder & CEO Vous Hotels & Retreats

"Be careful that you don't become married to your ideas. Love is blind and becoming married to your ideas makes you blind to possible outcomes and opportunities. Believe in what you're doing, but not to the point you are blinded by it. The only way to do this is to take action on your idea before you or the idea is "perfected."

Melissa Smith
Founder & CEO - Association of Virtual Assistants

"Build a strong network around you - it takes time and commitment but will bring great results for success and support in the years ahead."

Jacqui Frampton
Director – Concept Business Events

"Find something you enjoy doing and take great pride in the job."

Andrew Bailey
Governor - Bank of England

"Preparation is my word, both mentally and physically."

Jeff Fenech
World champion boxer in 3 weight divisions
and former trainer Mike Tyson

"When you have an idea, write it down, figure out why you want to do it, how you're going to do it. Then take action straight away because you could be procrastinating on an idea that could potentially change the world."

Holly Smith
BIZ FITNESS

*"If you can imagine it, you can achieve it!
+ 'Obsessed' is a word used by lazy people
to describe people who are goal-oriented."*

Professor Allan Pease
Chairman – Pease International

*"Keep on working for as long as you can. It keeps
your body and your brain functioning.
Surround yourself with young people - because they'll
help keep you young (in your head, anyway!)"*

Fred Dinage MBE
Television presenter, Broadcaster & Author

Pivotal Moment

The first pivotal moment in my life came after just after I'd left university. It was 1976, I was working at Maryvale Electronics delivering colour televisions. It was just before the Montreal Olympics, so we were very busy because it seemed as if everybody in Australia was getting a colour telly for the first time – as fast as the televisions came in, they were being sold, and I was part of the delivery team setting them up in new premises.

I got a call at about three o'clock on a Friday afternoon from someone who in time turned out to be my best man at my wedding – Greg Williams, a great guy. Greg said: 'John, we're all going on a cruise tomorrow.' To which I replied: 'Oh yeah, have a great time.' He said: 'The problem is that Chris [he's one of our mates] has just broken his leg only an hour ago.' And I said: 'Oh, okay. What's going to happen there?' And he said: 'Well, for obvious reasons, he won't be able to travel on the cruise. So do you think you could replace him if we could get them to agree?' And I said: 'Oh, okay. That sounds interesting.'

I went to my boss, Hans, and explained what had happened. And he thought about it for a second and even though we were busy, he asked me how long the cruise was for. I told him it was for two weeks and he said: 'And when would you be leaving?' I said: 'Tomorrow.'

I wouldn't have expected him to say yes, but he did, and on that cruise I met my first wife.

If that hadn't happened, my kids wouldn't have been born. My destiny wouldn't have been as it is today. Grandkids wouldn't have come along. It makes you stop and think on how innocuous moments can change your life.

Johnisms

Johnism 1

Which way are you looking?

There's a great reason why a windscreen's 40 times larger than a rear-vision mirror – you need to see a much bigger picture of where you're going. It means that 40 times out of 41 you're focused on looking forwards. But you still need to look backwards occasionally, just to reflect and learn the lessons of where you've been, but real action lies in front of you. Live your life as if you've got a windscreen that's 40 times larger than your rear-vision mirror.

Johnism 2

There's a movie I loved starring Dev Patel, The Best Exotic Marigold Hotel. It's set in India and he plays the hotel manager who comes out the best line ever: 'Everything will be all right in the end. If it's not all right, it is not yet the end.' Brilliant. It's a great line. Remember, if you're in a place where you think everything's imploding and falling down around, let me remind you that it will all be all right in the end. If it's not all right at the moment, then it can't be the end.

Johnism 3

Never let the 'how' stop the 'what'. So, you want to be in business? What business do you want to be in? What is it that you want to do? Don't worry about the 'how' at this stage – the nitty-gritty steps of getting from A to B – just concentrate on the 'what'. First, be clear about what you want and then apply yourself to how you are going to achieve it.

Johnisms

Chapter 2
Expect the unexpected

With the pilots strike in full swing and the car rental business in the balance I started looking at ideas to keep my life afloat.

A few months earlier we had seen a system in the United States in which businesses were getting together and operating their own bank-like operation. They were using a series of cheques and chequebooks with interest-free loan facilities in order to do business with each other by selling their spare capacity to the network and then appointing someone as a central banker to maintain the group.

This had the effect of connecting all those business owners in a very direct way so that they got to know one another. So, unlike a traditional bank, all the customers knew each other. They knew exactly who the other customers participating in the platform were.

This felt really interesting.

The platform offered interest-free credit lines to enable first purchases to take place, and so at any time the sum of the loans always equalled the sum of the deposits. It was what they called a 'debit-zero economy' – the purest form of banking there is. Whether it's called a pure bank, or a pure economy, or a pure money supply, it is what I believe to this day that every bank in the world or every economy should operate under.

It had to be worth a go.

So, I secured 50 business owners on the Gold Coast that were all friends from the car rental operation. These people were lawyers, accountants, marketing people, hoteliers , mechanics, retailers and others – they came from all walks of life. They got on board with the idea and we decided to start one of these business banks. I was appointed as the banker, and I was to be paid a commission on putting deals together and connecting people not fat fees irrespective of outcome or interest from lending money which was not theirs that traditional bankers made billions from.

My intuition told me that whilst I was still sorting out the car rental business, this was something I should be involved with.

It began, and, within a short period of time, we built a community. The pilot strike continued, and it took the then Prime Minister Bob Hawke to threaten commercial pilots that if they did not return to work on the next Monday, they'd all be sacked and they'd never fly a commercial aircraft in Australian airspace again! Hardball.

It had been going on for five months and, true to his word, that happened, the ones that didn't go back to work on Monday were sacked. I think about half of the striking pilots went back to work and so the industry began operating again, but the other half, to my knowledge, have never flown commercial aircraft again over Australian airspace.

A little bit like COVID, this was an unexpected event that you couldn't possibly forecast, that you couldn't see coming that smacked you in the face head on. A great Nugget I heard years later was a guy called Jeff Fenech who was a world boxing champion in three weight divisions and trained Mike Tyson, and he told me that Mike had said to him that everybody's got a plan until you get a smack in the face.

Genius!

Anyway, the business bank idea did very well and ten years later an opportunity arose with American Express to put together a large deal with 28 similar operations that I was reciprocally trading with around the world. We were well down the track into merging all those operations when 9/11 happened.

I got a little one-page message on my fax from the guy that we'd been dealing with for 18 months saying: 'In light of yesterday's tragic event, all operations are now ceased. This deal is now finished.' End of fax. We'd gone 18 months trying to put this massive deal together, and we were left with one paragraph on a fax machine. Having spoken to that guy every day for a year and a half, I've never ever spoken to him again since. It also shows the cold ruthlessness of vulture capitalists and huge corporations.

A Nugget teaching here is to always expect the unexpected!

However, as that door slammed shut in our faces another opened and a very opportunistic guy called Wayne Sharpe who'd started a company called Bartercard at the time came to me within a week and said: 'John, in light of what's happened, I believe your deal with American Express has fallen through. How would you like to merge into my company?'

And so, in a mixture of a scrip, cash, and trade currency, we sold our operation to Bartercard and became shareholders of that operation.

That deal brought me to the UK to start up the local operation. It was 2003. In 2011 we floated on the AIM, a sub-market of the London Stock Exchange.

After that I exited the business. As part of my exit agreement I had to stay out of the industry for a short period of time.

I went and worked for Microsoft. Again, that rekindled my experience with my man in the dole office because I hated working for an organisation that was so big that it didn't recognise any individual application. And I was really surprised because Microsoft is such a well-known and well-renowned business, you'd think that all their operations would be spot on, but I found myself in a situation where I was doing report decks every Friday and knowing that no one was reading them.

And I proved it because I put in a little message there that said: 'In my belief, we should change some of our marketing operations next week to add blue cows because, if we had blue cows they'd produce blue milk.'

When nobody mentioned anything about a week later when we had our meeting, I knew exactly that no one had read my report from last week. So it was just a box-ticking exercise in a multinational corporation where mid-level managers hide behind presentation decks and reports just to justify their existence and then send an email and copy the world to cover their ass, which was just such a ridiculous thing.

I thought: 'I never ever want to get back into that again. I want to continue in running my own business where I can make my own decisions, steer my own ship in the direction that I want to take it based on an educated guess as to where the end destination should look like but based on facts, based on experiences, and based on history that I'd learnt from talking to thousands of business owners over many years.'

One Nugget learning I take from the first part of my journey: Create a plan every time you undertake a new activity. Only with the benefit of hindsight was I to learn it. It has now become a golden rule.

Expect the unexpected

Business Blunders and Bloody Great Ideas

Let's share wisdom!

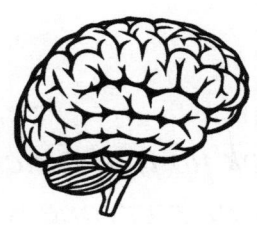

"Break the habits of a lifetime, be humble, discard pride and arrogance. TALK and really mean it."
Paul Bohill
TV personality & Debt collector extraordinaire

"Never look up to the rich, or down to the poor, treat everyone with the respect they deserve as a human being"
Ron Whitney
President - I.R.T.A.

"When it gets hard, or you feel stressed or overwhelmed, or you lose track of what you're doing, review your outcome.

What's the bigger picture?
What's the end goal?
What's the reason why behind that outcome.

The reason this is so effective is because it taps back into the passion you need to build a business. It's a tough slog, with bumps in the road and all sorts of crazy obstacles that show up - so when you focus back on where it is your going, it helps pave the way to get there."

Claire Byrne
Ned FD

"If you are arrested on charges of trying to be successful, would there be enough evidence to convict you?"

Dr Phil Jauncey
Performance Psychologist for elite sporting people and teams

"In the history of recorded time, no customer has ever said, 'Your price is too high,' and meant it."

Chuck Reeves
Speaker & Entrepreneur

"Your first wealth is your health meaning that if you fuel your body for success with an abundance to healthy food, you'll reach your business faster with your abundance of energy!

Barbara Cox-Lovesy
Nutritionist, Business Coach, Entrepreneur & Author

"Control your own destiny before someone else does."

Tony Brown
Retail Director

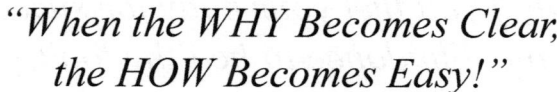

"When the WHY Becomes Clear, the HOW Becomes Easy!"

Keith Abraham
Speaker

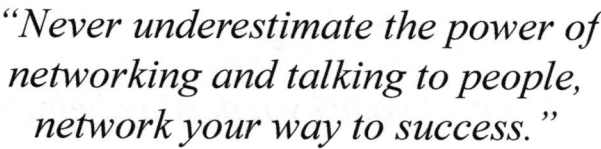

"Never underestimate the power of networking and talking to people, network your way to success."

Tracey Smolinski
Director & Founder – Introbiz (UK)

"If you have to eat shit, don't nibble!"

Warren Ostergard
Founder - Barter systems Cleveland

"Here is the harsh truth about life & business. Some folks will love you. Some will hate you. Some won't give two hoots for you. SO WHAT! Do the BEST you can anyway."

Trevor Nel
Founder - Wisdoms Group

Business Blunders and Bloody Great Ideas

Johnisms

Johnism 4

This is an adaptation of 'If you continue to do what you've always done, you'll always get what you've always got.' I think in this modern world, if you continue to do what you've always done, you'll not get what you've always got because the world is changing so quickly. So you've got to do things a little bit differently in order to get the change that you want in your life.

Johnism 5

Money is the most useless invention in history. Unless you obtain something that you need, beyond that it is greed. In other words, money for the sake of earning money is useless unless you buy something that you need.

Johnism 6

I remember back in the 1990s a taxi driver told me what the next 'hot topic' was. Believe me, by the time anything ever gets to the taxi driver, everybody's on it, and it's always the piece of knowledge that, really, you either know or you should know, or it's time to do something, or you should have done it already. So my mantra is when you hear of an opportunity from the taxi driver, it's time to act at 180 degrees. In other words, if the taxi driver's telling you to do it, it's time to do the complete opposite.

Johnisms

Business Blunders and Bloody Great Ideas

Chapter 3
Launching BBX

With the Microsoft experience firmly in the rear view mirror, a very enterprising young man called Michael Touma who founded BBX in 1993 in Sydney Australia contacted me on LinkedIn. He said: 'John, you're not in the industry any more. How would you like to start the branch of BBX here in the UK?'

This was 2013, and having known Michael for 20 years and worked with him before, I liked and trusted him. I thought: 'I like the idea. I like the concept.' I also knew that I didn't want to work for big corporations and although I really wasn't sure what I wanted to do, the other thing I knew for certain was that I wanted to do something I loved doing. Then, as now, I couldn't imagine ever working again on something that I didn't really love.

My time at Microsoft had taught me some valuable lessons – the Nugget here is that you can be on a massive salary with a great benefits package, but if you don't really love it, nothing is worth the job dissatisfaction.

Anyway, suitably intrigued by Michael's suggestion I jumped on a plane and went down to Sydney to catch up with him. He'd built an active and varied network and was the trailblazer at the forefront of that organisation, a true beacon of light, and it didn't take long for us to reach an agreement where I could set up a license to run the UK operation of BBX, on a 90-year agreement. The reason I liked the deal was that BBX already had thousands of customers in other countries in all parts of the world.

BBX was a system of digital trade credits operating very much like my Queensland trade exchange with chequebooks and analogue systems, but BBX had developed an online platform that used bank-like software with apps for companies to transact between one another. Effectively, BBX brought my old platform into the digital age.

The whole concept of BBX was having a community of business owners that were like-minded in that they had three problems to solve. Either wanted to grow their business, get a better lifestyle from running the business, or to sell it for more at the end of a given period of time. Business is a lonely place at times, but with BBX adding in events and a sense of community and connections it seemed to me like the ideal solution.

I opened up the UK branch and got together with Scott Clancy and Matthew Harding who I'd worked with previously. Each of them had different expertise, and I go back to my earlier Nugget that whatever business you lead, you need great people around you – people that are as passionate about and love the project as much as you do. If everybody in the business is immersed in the same concept, the same flow, then you have a much better chance of success.

That said, I have to admit I really envy those lucky souls that can do it all on their own – let's call them 'solopreneurs'. It's one person doing everything and going after their vision. I admire that greatly, but it's not my way. I could never work like that. I need to have people behind me sweeping up all the chaos that I create from starting various projects. If it's just left for me to do it, I'd end up with a whole lot of ideas that start but are never seen through to fruition. People like me need the sweepers behind making sure all the t's are crossed and the i's are dotted.

A Nugget here is: Know what you're good at and focus on making that better.

Matthew is a master of franchising and sales, that's his passion, and I'd trained Scott on the trading side of the business, connecting business owners with account managers that call every single one of our clients on a regular basis to stimulate and uncover spare capacity as well as help them spend that money once they've earned it. It's a great business to be in if you're an account manager, helping people make money and then helping them spend it as well –

the perfect 360-degree operation. I don't know that you get all the joy from the outcome of the spend, but you see what happens and see what you've created, and that in itself is a joyful position.

BBX helps people in business capture and monetise previously worthless spare capacity in their business. One of the things that I speak regularly about all over the world is doing something with spare capacity because, at the moment, most people in business still don't calculate their spare capacity. To be frank, a lot of the time they don't even know what I'm talking about when I first encounter them. So, not only do they not calculate and monetise spare capacity, they don't do anything with it.

I encourage everybody with spare capacity to at least try to do something with it. Take a hotel as an example. Say you owned a hotel with 100 rooms and you sold every room for £100 a night. If you had 50% occupancy, you'd have a pretty decent business. You'd be earning £5,000 a night, you'd be paying all your overheads, and you'd have a more than reasonable revenue for yourself.

But then I come in and challenge that business owner. What did they do with the 50 rooms that weren't sold last night? Let's calculate the value of that. How much are they missing out on? There are 50 rooms, each of them worth £100 a night. That's £5,000 a night. If the hotel is trading every night of the year that's £5,000 a night times 365 nights. That's £1.825 million in unsold capacity and I ask them what they did with it last year. Typically, at this point I get a look of shock and horror on the face of the business owner. They usually say something along the lines of they did nothing with it. If something could have been done they'd have done it.

In fairness that's probably true. Running a business is hugely demanding and you can't be over everything at once – again proving my Nugget about having great people around you.

But let's look at the structure of that business and ask the hotel owner what costs are incurred as a result of not selling that spare capacity. They'd probably conclude that there are no additional costs to spare capacity – the wages are paid, the maintenance is paid, rates, marketing, running costs are all paid and they're still making a profit even though there is spare capacity in the business.

Fair enough, but consider this. If one of those unsold rooms were sold into the BBX community, what costs would increase? The hotel receptionist doesn't get paid more, the rates are the same, as are maintenance and marketing. All it would cost the hotel owner is a bar of soap, a squirt of shampoo, egg and bacon for breakfast, plus a fee for BBX and when that is looked as a multiple, it's never more than about £20 - 20%

In other words, to make £100, a spare capacity sale might only cost the hotel owner £20 because none of the fixed costs rise. When sold into the BBX community the hotel has earned 100 digital trade credits without any of my static fixed costs going up or down. They still have their £5,000 coming in, that hasn't changed, but they've turned an empty bedroom into some held value at a cost of about £20.

Our hotel owner has 100 digital trade credits in a separate account at a cost of £20 to acquire. Let's say they then decide to go and buy £100 worth of window cleaning. Now, instead of paying £100 cash for the window cleaning, he gets a fellow participant of the BBX community who cleans windows to do the work using their 100 digital trade credits that funded by what was previously an empty bedroom !

So, what's changed? Well, if you think, the windows are still being cleaned, all things being equal, but, instead of having to pay £100 out of cash flow to clean the windows, the hotel is, in effect, only paying £20 being for the peripheral costs and my fee to earn the £100 in the first place. So, the hotel owner has now been able to add £80 to the bottom line bottom-line profit.

But let's see what else has happened? The empty bedroom was occupied and, if the person that stayed in the room liked the room, they might tell their friends. What's more, if they weren't previously a part of the BBX community that could lead to extra cash business coming in the front door. Can an empty bed give a referral?

What's more, this new customer stayed at our hotel not a competitor's and there's nothing wrong with taking a bit of business off a rival. Imagine if they had actually liked the competitor's hotel – how much business might that have lost our owner? Think about it, how many times have you had to go somewhere else because the place you usually go to is closed, out of stock, closed down, or whatever? You've always bought your widget at Mary's place, but Mary was closed today so you went down to Mary's competitor and bought the widget there. Perhaps you thought: 'Oh, wow. These widgets aren't so bad.' Suddenly, there's a chance you won't go back to Mary's next time.

And there we have it – the marketing advantages of doing something with some spare capacity rather than letting it go to waste. You can add them to the financial advantages accrued from buying profit with a discount equivalent to your gross margin. In other words, in my example, it has cost you just £20 to buy £100 worth of window cleaning.

The final benefit is that it adds strength to your balance sheet because the BBX revenue counts one for one for EBITDA – that's Earnings Before Interest, Taxes, Depreciation, and Amortisation and is a measure of a company's overall performance before the effects of interest, taxes and costs. Essentially, is demonstrates a stronger balance sheet, meaning you'll improve the lending opportunities of the business if you need to loan traditional funds. And, if you go to sell the business at any point in the future, you'll have additional revenue to help increase the sale price of the business.

Let's share wisdom!

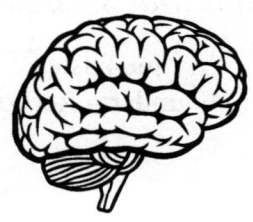

"Believe in your product or service 100% because if you don't believe then no-one else will. And then build a team that shares your belief."

Joe Foster
Founder – Reebok

"Determine the non-negotiables for success... Execute Them Daily!"

Joe Pici
Sales Master

"You never get a second chance to create a good first impression."

John Parrett
Owner - Fox Tailoring

"When it's delivered correctly, sales and customer service are EXACTLY the same thing."

Alison Edgar MBE
Sales expert, author and keynote speaker

"AFTERs drive everything. In other words customers don't care what you do. Instead, they want why they're better-off AFTER it.

- *We don't want IT; we want quicker, virtual working*
- *We don't want marketing; we want more leads*
- *We don't want a drill; we want a hole*
- *And your customers don't want you. But they do want..."*

Andy Bounds
Keynote speaker & author

"If you want to raise productivity in any business or group all you have to do is Raise Responsibility Levels - do that so the whole team feels they own everything that happens and the statistics will just keep on rising!!!"

Andrew Banks
Chairman Veneto Group - Sharks Tank Australia

"Don't over-complicate things. Business is simply the art of persuading others to transfer money from their bank accounts into yours."

Gill Bevis
Owner – The Business Magazine

"Be Yourself - to often and especially when presenting we feel the need to adopt an alter ego, a slick persona, that we think the audience, the team need to hear from. When we accept that the real version of ourselves, with the natural imperfections we all exhibit is in fact the person the audience really wants to hear from, then we can relax and be the best version of our real selves on the day."

Andy Taylor – Whyte
Charity fundraising expert

"Profitability is created by professional dedication (pro) to well founded (fit) use of talent (ability)."

Barry Cusack
Former MD - Rio Tinto Australia
$450 billion shareholder value company & President of Minerals Council of Australia

"God made us with two ears and one mouth. A great leader listens more than he talks."

Steve Legg
Founder & CEO - Sorted magazine

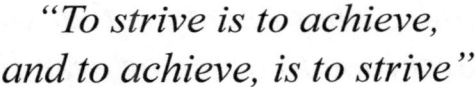

*"To strive is to achieve,
and to achieve, is to strive"*

Unisa Kamara
TV host & speaker

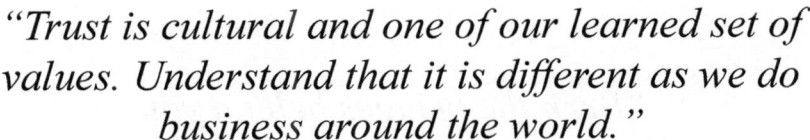

"Trust is cultural and one of our learned set of values. Understand that it is different as we do business around the world."

Steve Williams
Mining leader 4 decades

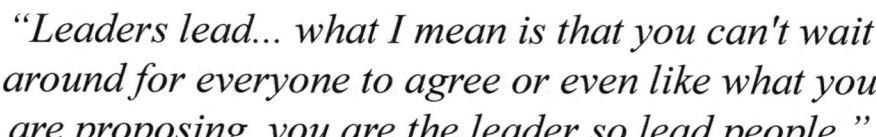

"Leaders lead... what I mean is that you can't wait around for everyone to agree or even like what you are proposing, you are the leader so lead people."

Angela De Souza
CEO - Women's Business Club

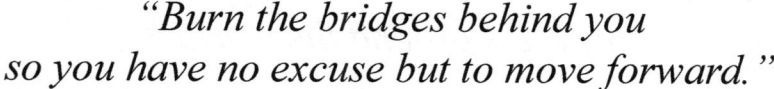

"Burn the bridges behind you so you have no excuse but to move forward."

Steve Jones
Business & motivational leadership trainer

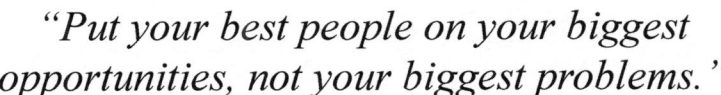

"Put your best people on your biggest opportunities, not your biggest problems."

Tim Bishop
Senior partner law firm

"Customer feedback is important – but it's not their job to imagine the future. Listen to feedback, listen or ideally see the problems with what they're doing currently – but often you'll need to show them what's possible before they can say if they want it. And to give an example of that as Henry Ford said - If I had asked customers what they wanted they would have told me a faster horse."

Tom Ball
Founder and pioneer flexible work spaces

Johnisms

Johnism 7

Who do you look for in a business partner?

Some people like to go it alone, but I challenge those people because most people are great at either sales and marketing, or product type innovation. Peter Drucker mentions that only about 8% of entrepreneurs are sales and marketing led and some 92% are product-based entrepreneurs. I challenge all the sales-based entrepreneurs, who are incidentally disproportionately more successful than the product-led entrepreneurs.

The reason is that a sales-led entrepreneur goes out there and creates havoc in the marketplace, signs up new customers. Unless they have got a product-based or a more 'dot i, cross t' business partner behind them, cleaning up all the stuff, delivering the customer service, delivering the product, all the boring stuff that the sales-based entrepreneur doesn't like and is not good at, then the business probably won't be as successful as if you have a combination of two.

On the flip side of that, if you've only got a product-led entrepreneur, nine times out of 10 they struggle with one big thing and that's getting new customers. So, I've seen some great businesses over the years that have had a great product, great idea, and the person behind them is great at understanding the technical knowledge, how it works, but they're no good at what it does.

So here's a Nugget: Build your team purposefully; know who you are and who else you need around you. And never let the how people stop the what people – in other words if you come up with a great idea work out how to do it as you go.

Johnism 8

My next Johnism is from my old business partner David Johnstone. David and I worked together for 13 years. We sold that business and we're lifelong friends. His thing was having to deal with people that are all waffle, no action. He described them as 'All fart, no shit.' And that encapsulates a lot of people that you run across. If you bear that in mind, then you can ignore them and simply move on.

Johnism 9

We all know the old adage: 'If it ain't broke, don't fix it'. But, if it is not working, you have to change it – and quickly. Procrastination over doing things is one of the worst things that can beset either a businessperson or something in your life. And you'll be thinking about something, and you'll ponder it for ages and ages and ages. You'll finally make the decision and think: 'Jeez, why didn't I just do that six months ago?' So, make decisions quickly because, generally speaking, they're the right ones. So if it's not broken, don't mend it, but if it is, put it right as quickly as possible.

Business Blunders and Bloody Great Ideas

Chapter 4
Growing BBX

You'll recall what I said about expecting the unexpected…

A week after starting the UK operation of BBX with two people that I'd worked with in the previous business we got a writ on a cease and desist order saying that I had poached these people from other businesses and it was against their work contracts. Great. The business was barely a week old and already it had the threat of legal action hanging over it.

I jumped on the phone to BBX founder, my old mate Michael Touma, reasoning that BBX was a global operation so he had probably dealt with this kind of thing before and would have some sensible, reasonable, legally-conscious advise for me on how to this unwelcome turn of events.

His response? 'Tell them to go f*** themselves!'

Fair enough – can't be any clearer than that!

Anyway, we ploughed on through that and managed to set up the exchange. I then reached out to the best administration person I knew – my wife.

My advice to anyone who starts a business would to get somebody very close to you to look after the pennies because I've seen a lot of business owners who don't or can't take care of the money properly and abdicate the responsibility to someone not so close to them only to find to their cost that it doesn't always work out as well as they hoped.

Having overcome the various obstacles that were put in our way, we were finally up and running with a small core team of people I knew well and trusted implicitly. Looking back now it was a very proud moment and, although I didn't realise it back then, the beginning of something incredibly special that would go on to change my life.

For the first year, to keep our overheads in check, we operated out of the office above the sign shop – although we were focused on sales, customer service and the administrative backup, we also wanted to mitigate overhead. At this stage with my wife in the admin area we only needed someone else very part-time, they were the only person on a salary. Everyone else in the business became a shareholder so instead of one person hogging it all and promising the key partners a five or ten per cent share in years to come, we almost became equal shareholders.

Now, someone on the outside looking in might think: 'Well, John, you're the key operator in the business. You're the instigator. You're the one that found the deal. You're the one that set it up. Why aren't you the majority shareholder?'

My response to that is I'd rather have key people with good skin in the game that are operating with me because, that way, the sum of the parts becomes greater than the whole. And so it has proved to be – we started up on that basis and the shareholding hasn't changed to this day.

Our first task was to establish a client base, not least because if you don't have clients then you don't have revenue and if you don't have revenue you can't pay your bills and you don't have a business. Without a big wad of money behind us we had to make sure pretty quickly that the business was focused on finding, cultivating retaining clients. It's obvious, but you'd be surprised how many businesses I know of that focus on too many other, less important things.

We started off with share capital with the three of us putting in £5,000 each and since that day we've never made another contribution and we've never borrowed any money. We've always been self-funded and we've always made sales to cover our costs. That's something I'm particularly proud of.

Being a sales-led organization – and here's another Nugget for you – you can always sell yourself out of any financial issue if you have a sales led focus. All you've got to do is make more sales. Simple, right?

Well, not necessarily. There are so many businesses out there that might be great at selling their products – let's say they're a great shoe seller – but what happens when something unexpected happens and (pardon the pun) footfall drops off. If their only strategy had been to make sales to customers that come through the door the business could be in trouble.

Put another way, if you don't have a fully thought out sales strategy, how can you turn the tap on when you need to? The thing with BBX is that we can always make more sales because there are always businesses out there with spare capacity that we haven't met yet. If we need to boost sales we simply move our focus to approaching businesses with spare capacity that are not currently in the network and generate more revenue in the front door. That creates additional revenue streams via the trading mechanism.

When we set up BBX we wanted multiple revenue streams to spread the source of business income rather than put all our eggs in one or two baskets. We started with four different revenue streams, and not only are they different revenue streams, but they are also repeatable.

Once we'd earned the money, we were setting up a monthly recurring fee for services based on a one-time sale. So, we made the sale once, but we got the revenue monthly. Building up new customers month by month meant that over time we were getting more and more monthly revenue from the six months, five months, four months, three months, two months, and the current month's sales activity. Any business that's only as good as its last sale is also a very fractured structure. Making sales that you can get repeatable revenue from rather than just one-time customers is a strategy that I talk about and advocate for wholeheartedly.

After a few months trading we'd done deals and had a big focus. We had secured around 500 clients and we had enough revenue to pay the directors and we moved into our first franchise.

As is often the case with my closest business associates I'd worked with Ben Jacob previously. He was our first franchisee and what I'd call a reluctant entrepreneur – he'd had enough of working for someone else, but was not completely sold on the idea of going it alone either. There are so many people who fall into this category. I speak around the world on franchising and licensing, and I've met many a great franchisee who is sick and tired of being a P-A-Y-E person earning the same money irrespective of the effort they put in every month, but lacking the vital spark it takes to completely abandon that safety net.

Finding the right franchisee for your business is not an easy thing to do. You don't want someone who's just going to take everything they learn about your business then starting up in competition to you, but if you get someone who is stuck in a P-A-Y-E mentality then they'll never run their own business because they'll just sit there and not be as committed as every business owner has to be.

Matthew Harding was in charge of recruiting franchisees and after 12 months we had two franchisees. A year later we had four franchisees and we built that model all the way through. After the first five years, we had a dozen franchisees – ten in the UK and two in Ireland.

Bearing in mind I'm Australian and used to big distances and wide open territory, this was nothing. People here say the UK is a big place, but the UK is about the same size as the Aussie state of Victoria and if you understand what Australia looks like, Victoria is the little itty-bitty state down the bottom. To my way of thinking at least, the UK is tiny.

But anyway, after five years we had franchisees in Newcastle, up in Scotland, down in Devon, London, Northampton, on the coast down base here in Bournemouth where our Head Office is, and then over in Ireland in Cork and Dublin. At that point we were up to about 8,000 clients in the UK, but replicating the model by having other people that were following our action plan under the franchising model.

We helped the Approved Franchise Association get off the ground and we remain strong supporters of that organisation. For anybody who's into franchising, I'd recommend becoming part of an Approved Franchise Association structure of some kind, whatever that is, wherever that is.

Walk Your Talk!

At the time I started BBX I was a non-executive owner of a wide-format sign-and-print business. Upstairs in that business, there was a big room that wasn't used. And so, the first BBX office was created in what had been an empty space, turning some spare capacity in that sign-and-print business into some value for another project in my armoury.

Let's share wisdom!

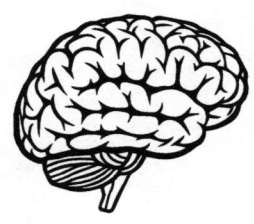

"John, a nugget that springs to mind was the time you told me 'always be recruiting even when you don't need to be' which I have stuck by since and the 'gaps' I used to have with staff movement are a lot less."

Will Bellows
Business owner & IT expert

"Do what you enjoy and are really good at that people will pay you to do. "

Tony Robinson OBE
Small business champion & author

"In any commercial trade exchange or other credit clearing system, it is the pledge of the producer members (participants) to provide valued goods and services that give the trade credits value; that is why credit lines must be properly allocated in proportion to each member's ability and willingness to provide what people want and need, and accept trade credits as payment. The amount of credit allocated to each producer/seller is in no way a judgment about their personal worth or trustworthiness, rather it is the "monetization" of the value of the goods or services that is each producer is ready, willing, and able to sell in the immediate time-frame."

Tom Greco
Associate Professor & private currency expert of 56 years

"In today's world, innovation only becomes disruption when users adopt it, so, rather than striving to disrupt the system, think about how you can be useful to people in this moment."

William Sachiti
Founder - Institute of Robotics

"Culture eats strategy for breakfast, lunch and dinner – don't leave it to chance."

Susan Gruenwald
President - Emerita Chamberlain University
& Trade exchange founder

"Change doesn't have to be big, it just has to be positive."

Lizzie McManus
Warrior Agency PR

"The difference between success and failure is determination, commitment, and hard work."

Steve Bicknell
Accounting expert

"It's never about you, it's always about them. Take price objections for example. You are not too expensive: they're either not the right client or they don't fully understand the outcomes you'll create."

Steve McKenna
Media entrepreneur

"Don't let anyone underestimate you if you have a goal or passion. They may be further up the ladder than you, looking down, but you'll soon meet them on your way up – and they will meet you on their way down."

Janet Kelly
Media entrepreneur

"Change should never be feared, but embraced in all its glory."

Rick Powell
Commentator - Sky Sports

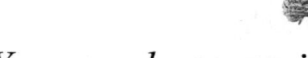

"You may have aspirations of greatness but you will not bask in success you don't believe you can achieve."

Kevin Byrne
Founder – Checkatrade

"CFO to CEO: What happens if we invest in training our people- and they leave?

CEO reply : Think about what happens if we don't - and they stay!"

Michael Trigg
The Presentation Maestro

"Lead, follow or get out of the way."

Craig Duffy
Entrepreneur and former Australian champion
professional snooker and pool player

*"As a Leader, it's not about being in charge,
it's about taking care of the people in your charge."*

Chanelle McCoy
Dragons Den Ireland

"Everyone can be an overnight success if you were to wake up each new day a little smarter, a litter wiser, and little stronger than the day before."

Brian Esposito
Founder – Esposito Intellectual Enterprises

"Knowing yourself puts you in a position of power in life and in business. It will free you of life's bullies; especially the bully of other people's opinion!"

Bernie Davies
Publisher author TEDx speaker and International master coach

"The key to success in baseball (as well as any other endeavour, I believe) is mental, and until you believe you are good enough to compete you won't, regardless of your physical skills."

Bob Meyer
New York Yankees Editor - Barter News

"Don't tolerate egoists in your organization. Whatever accomplishments they bring are always less than the damage they will do."

Chong Kee Tan
Farmer - Labishire Farms

Business Blunders and Bloody Great Ideas

Johnisms

Johnism 10

Mental health, people say: 'John, how come you've never got have any issues with life or anything that goes on around your life?' For me it all comes back to the old Bobby McFerrin song, 'Don't Worry, Be Happy'. If you are unhappy, do something about it. Right now. If you can't control the outcome, then ignore it because worry is not going to help it. So, I always live my life by the maxim that if I can't change something, I don't have any control over it; and I can't put anything in place to change the outcome, then there's absolutely no point worrying about it because that won't change a thing. That's why I sleep so soundly every single night.

Johnism 11

Recruit people for their attitude. You can train aptitude, and the right people with the right attitude become great people. Don't just look for skill sets when you're recruiting people, have a good look at their attitude. Ask questions around attitude. Are they competitive? Are they willing to learn? Are they nice people? Are they genuine? If they are, you can always train that type of person to match the skill set required for the role. Lastly always be recruiting – especially when you don't need to – that way you don't make panic appointments.

Johnism 12

In my experience, you need to spend between seven and 11% of your turnover on getting your business, your product or services known. If you're not spending that much on sponsorship, promotion, PR, advertising, marketing, all things web-based, then you're not giving your business the fuel it deserves in order to be a success. You wouldn't expect to drive a car without fuel to power it so treat your business like a car and put some gas/diesel/electric in the tank. You need to spend around 80% of those revenues on existing customers – something I learned from Kevin Byrne, founder of Checkatrade.com. The Nugget he passed on to me was to spend 80% of your marketing budget on customers you already have because they will drive a far better result than if you spend the same amount trying to attract new customers, people that you don't even know.

Chapter 5
Growth can kill you!

Growing a business is not only one of the joys of working for yourself it's essential for the future health of the business. You can never stand still. We wanted to get bigger quicker.

Then we had a brainwave – we'd bring on lumps of people in clusters. Up until that point our sales structure relied on a sales person making a one-to-one sale – one person talking to another person, belly to belly, replicating the information and hopefully getting them to sign onto the system.

Now that's a well-tried and tested method of attracting business, but it's also incredibly time consuming, and very labour intensive. This idea lead us to a guy called Warren Cass who had the Champions of Small Business, and he had 24,000 businesses that subscribed to his system. We sent them all an email saying this is what BBX does and if anybody in the Champions of Small Business wanted to come along, we'd let them join for a pound, as a value add for the work that Warren was doing with the Champions of Small Business.

Lo and behold, 1,081 people responded and opted in. Amazing!

When we started BBX there was approximately 5.2 million businesses in the UK and we thought fairly if we could get a 10% market share that would remove 90% of the competition. If you had ten hotels in one town and one was on BBX, the other nine weren't, that'd be 10% of the population. That'd be a great community of half a million people. So that was our goal. But we were five years in and only at 5,000 so we figured out that we're never going to get to our goal at the rate. We had to do something differently.

And this was working. We brought these 1,081 new customers aboard with bells singing. So much that we went out for beers that night and toasted a glass or many to our success – we thought that it was the greatest deal ever. Even the history of BBX, no one had ever done that number of new customers in one month and Michael Touma was congratulating us. Everything else was going great as well – by this time we'd moved out of the sign business premises and got our own office in the centre of Bournemouth, a much bigger office.

Then all hell broke loose!

Funny that, but it happens a lot in business. Just when you think you've made your life simpler and more successful things get a load more complicated and you're staring into the abyss yet again.

We were getting a lot of complaints from our account managers all moaning and groaning because every single client needed to have an installation meeting and all their time was being taken up settling in new clients. Because BBX represents a different type of product we had to sit down and go through the business with each and every new client to make sure they understand exactly what it is that they've bought. For the BBX community to work properly each new client needs to know what it does and doesn't do, what it can and can't do, the sorts of businesses that you can deal with and the ones that'll never ever deal with us, not because the concept doesn't make sense, but because you can never get to the decision maker.

In short, we had made a rod for our back. Our trading volume went from doing really well to plummeting because all the account managers were fully focused, and they had to be, on on-boarding this tsunami of new clients.

And when I say tsunami, we had a 20% increase in customers in one deal. Now that's all right if you've only got a few customers, but when you had 5,000 and you're getting another 1,000 then it just represented such an issue and we suffered from that for the better part of 12 months until we got those new people settled.

The downside was because they are all lumped in and only paid a pound to become part of BBX they didn't have the buy-in with the people that have paid a £1,000 or, in some cases, £4,000. Scaling became such an issue for us that even today we haven't solved it completely, but we are working on it!

The Nugget here is to be careful what you wish for. This situation almost sent us down because all our focus had to be on the new customers and the old customers were quite rightly putting their hands up saying: "Hey, what about me?'

Sometimes the great opportunity is actually a wolf in sheep's in clothing, so to speak.

All that drama took us through the better part of 2018, which turned out to be our best year to date. We'd built up to about 8,000 customers by that point in the UK, and things were going pretty sweet.

The new year, 2019, arrived and we found ourselves in the situation where some of our activity had plateaued. This is the next stage in growing a business. We'd had that first rush of momentum and then hit a sudden upward curve of rapid growth before reaching a point where at 8,000 customers it levelled out.

By the time we hit 8,000 customers, by the natural law of business we could reasonably expect to lose probably 1% every month. That's 80 customers, so if we weren't on-boarding 160 new customers every month, we weren't growing. Itmwas fine back at the start when we had 100 customers and were bringing on 50 in a month, that's a great number, but when you're at 8,000, unless you're scaling your sales operation, then you can't scale faster than you lose through attrition.

Every business gets to this curve where attrition meets new sale numbers and when that happens the business will plateau. There's a mathematical formula for doing that and I don't care what business it is, you get to a point where if you can't scale up your sales operation, you will plateau.

As ever, the solution lies in how you respond.

Business Blunders and Bloody Great Ideas

Let's share wisdom!

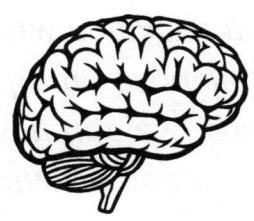

"As soon as we individually realise that business is personal, we take back control over our life, our ambitions, our personal drivers and our own levels of resilience and desires. Modern communication through social media has reduced many to believe that we have to be and do what others are, yet, how can we, we all have very different needs, life experiences, ambitions and abilities to sacrifice what it takes. Layer passion and purpose on top, as well as you current life needs, we can never be like anyone else. Happiness comes when we take back control of our own business plan and live our life the way it works for us, personally."

Penny Power OBE
Founder Ecademy, author, keynote speaker & chat show host

"My drive in life is to create a positive presence that has presence when I am not present!"
Richard Flint
Author, keynote speaker, trainer and coach

"Look to introduce and use as much technology as possible, to reduce human input and create as much efficiency as possible, this would include using the Audible app."
Michael Chittenden
Property Entrepreneur

"Your attitude determines you altitude."

Mel Fisher
Chief Opportunity Advisor - Business For Breakfast

"It doesn't matter how many times you try and fail, it matters how many times you are willing to get up, dust yourself off and try again. Whether you are the next Thomas Edison, or the next Elon Musk, remember, you have to fail to learn, learn to fail and most importantly, get up and take decisive action."

Martin Tindall
Cannabis Entrepreneur

"I have two ears and one mouth, make sure they are used in proportion."

David Johnstone
Board member and chair of 5 companies over $200 million turnover

"You can have anything in life you want, if you just help other people get what they want."

Dominic Ricciardi
Property & cryptocurrency investor and entrepreneur

"When you've made a decision about hiring or firing a new supplier of colleague then do it straight away – don't wait – the compound effect of waiting can be very costly indeed."

Nigel Apperley
Founder - Trustist

"Who you're working with is much more important than what you're working on. Every successful business requires a great idea and a well-executed plan, but even the most star-studded roster will fail if they don't gel as a team."

Scott Parazynski
Astronaut

"If it's to be its up to me!"

Scott Fitzpatrick
Elite sports family & wealth management expert

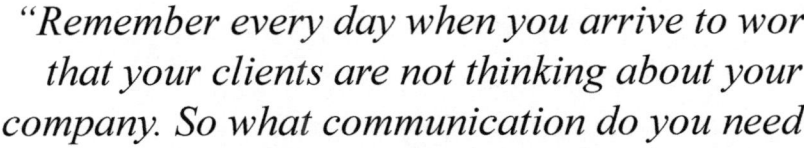

"Remember every day when you arrive to work, that your clients are not thinking about your company. So what communication do you need to do to stay relevant and have your clients thinking about you. A phone call goes a long way!"

Scott Whitmer
IRTA Hall of Fame

"I learned a long time ago to keep my email inbox to an absolute minimum (I have 28 at the moment!). To do this I dedicate a time to purely focus on them (three or four times a day) and then Deal (reply straight away - even if it's to say I'll reply more fully later), Delete, Delegate or File in specific folders."

Alistair Greener
Event host MC and Moderator

"Don't forget when building a business to grow your soul as well as your bank balance."

Darryl Bannon
Business mentor

"You will always be bombarded by multiple vultures, with the offers of either:

- *Guru's words of wisdom & experience*
- *Networking group opportunities offering the very best in connections*
- *+ so many more*

My Advice is, always do your research on all those that prey on start-ups.

- *Guru's - Check their LinkedIn profile on how many so-called businesses they've Owned/Managed & to what level. You will find most have managed ......SFA other than read a book*
- *Network Groups - Do your research on existing members & businesses - Most you will find irrelevant, one-man bands, small businesses, multiple of, full of non-decision makers & too costly."*

Marc Ferguson
Sporting events entrepreneur

"If you were dissected you would bleed whatever business you were working in at that time."

Mike Perry
Publican & golfing legend

"Some habits simply don't scale. In fact, some habits become toxic when they become larger! You must observe the habits of your life and discard them when they stop you from reaching the next level of your potential."

Malcolm Larri
TEDx host

A Nugget I learned from my parents.

I guess not everybody's as lucky as I am to have had a mother and father that were loving. They were together and worked together in their own business.

That was always my grounding and anybody who has parents that have been in their own business gets to understand a lot more as to how a business operates. My father and my mother were such hard workers. They milked cows for a better part of 20 years, twice a day, hardly ever had a holiday. I remember going on holiday with them just once when I was a kid because they were working all the time. They were committed, to the point where they were in their forties when they retired. They sold the farm for a lot more than what it was when they bought it.

That gave them enough money to work part time when they wanted to, not when they needed to.

And so my parents played a big part in my life. They didn't pay for everything, but I was never given anything. I was given the foundation, but I was taught that I had to work for whatever it is that I wanted to get.

I used to do work on the farm. I started off with about sixpence an hour, which was nothing back in those days, but it taught me the ethic of work, the ethic of doing something for something. And for that, I owe my parents a great deal of gratitude.

Business Blunders and Bloody Great Ideas

Johnisms

Johnism 13

When we are looking for new customers, there are three groups of people – Suspects, Prospects and Insects. Let me explain – imagine you are driving along a dusty road, it hasn't rained for sometime and the bugs have been coming down on your windscreen. Then, all of a sudden, you get a shower of rain and you put your wipers on, and the next thing you have is a windscreen smeared with bugs – you can't see where you're going. I liken that to prospecting in sales. Your Suspects are those people who you don't yet know whether they're actual Prospects that might become real clients, or Insects that will splatter against your windscreen. Add a little water and you can't see where you're going, but give it a good wash and you'll soon see where you're going. So, you need to really focus in order to maintain your direction. Don't be put off by the Insects that mess up your screen, the worse they can do is cloud your vision – wash them down be on your way, looking for more of the proper Prospects.

Johnism 14

When you're making an innovation of some kind, make sure you keep your Finance Director and your Chief Technology Officer locked in a dark cupboard! You want to break the mold, take a few risks and push boundaries, but those guys are the ones who are dedicated to dotting Is and crossing Ts. They have many great qualities that your business cannot do without, but they can be the enemies of innovation. So, let's keep them in the dark cupboard while we try to innovate and drive the business forward.

Johnism 15

Do something with spare capacity. I run across people all the time, brilliant people that have run businesses big and small. They're great on their figures. They're great on their P&L. They're great on their balance sheet. But they've never stopped and calculated the spare capacity in their business. It's so simple. It's a calculation that will determine what is the potential revenue in your business that you haven't spent any time looking for, or monitoring, or trying to figure out how to do something with. Spare capacity can be monetised and turned into revenue. Speak to my team at BBX, they can help.

Business Blunders and Bloody Great Ideas

Chapter 6
Learn from history

Having reached that plateau in 2019, our big question was: 'How can we get this thing to the next level?'

The answer was to bring on-board Alex Clapcott. Alex is a sales and marketing guru with a very strong background in membership organisations. I first met Alex back in 2014 when I was still in the sign business and he delivered a keynote presentation at an event that I'd gone to. I was impressed and had kept in touch, speaking to Alex on and off over the years.

But when I reached out to Alex at the start of 2020 none of us could have foreseen the thing that would stand in our way. Covid.

It goes without saying that, as it did everywhere, Covid had a massive impact on our business. I'll never forget the day we went into lockdown in March 2020. All of a sudden, literally overnight, we were unable to operate. Our salespeople couldn't go belly to belly with new prospects. The account managers couldn't work from the office. And for a business whose environment is that of a buzzy office where people bounce off one another that's bad news. The 2020 version of the 1989 pilots strike ! Funny how history has a habit of repeating itself – just a little nudge to those who want to erase it!

We have bells that go off when something decent happens in the organisation because I'm a strong believer in celebrating success and a little bell or something to mark the moment tells everybody that a good thing has just happened. It gives everyone a little lift and the more times the bell goes off, the more times the bell goes off… that's what I've found by celebrating success!

But all of that disappeared in an instant when everybody had to be locked down and work from home. What the hell were we going to do?

Like most sales and marketing entrepreneurs, we had a strategy meeting and I reached deep into to my memory box and dug out another thing that I strongly believe in and understand and work with… it's called the Pareto Principle, or 80/20 Principle.

I was on a plane going to America one time, and I got a book called The 80/20 Principle: The Secret of Achieving More with Less by Richard Koch. I'd recommend it to anybody. It's an easy read and I was through it in a couple of hours. The Pareto Principle states that for many outcomes roughly 80% of consequences come from 20% of causes. This has stuck with me ever since. Put another way, 80% of your rewards come from 20% of your efforts. Or another, 80% of your customers do nothing; so 20% of your customers are responsible for 80% of your turnover.

Written in 1997 – pre-internet for most of us – it's an interesting read and has remained true to this day. It might surprise some but the internet hasn't changed the 80/20 world.

Our challenge was how to survive the Covid pandemic because if we didn't do something, there'd be no customers left there when we came out of it. Most of our clients' businesses were in the same boat – they were unable to trade. If their businesses closed, they can't trade. If they can't trade, they don't have any revenue and if they don't have any revenue, neither does BBX. And if BBX doesn't have any revenue, we don't have a business.

What a great challenge to rise to! We locked ourselves up for three days and nights to work out the strategies to put in place in order to overcome this adversity using the Pareto Principle. In essence it boiled down to this – with the account managers working remotely, we decided to focus our attention on the 20% of customers that deliver 80% of our revenue.

At that time from our 8,000 customers, we whittled it down to about 1,600 who delivered the bulk of our income. They were the ones we needed to focus on. We contacted the others to explain that although we would call every now and then, for the time being, for the next three months at least, we had to focus on the customers that deliver the greatest portion of our revenue.

It proved to be a winning formula. It saved us. Absolutely.

What we were able to do during Covid was to balance the ship and we're thankful for that. A lot of people blame governments and leaders and, frankly, anyone other than themselves for their failure, but most of the failure that occurs with those people looks back at them in the mirror every morning when they get up.

It's a great expression, but when the going gets tough, the tough get going. And by focusing on the 20% of customers that delivered us 80% of the revenue, we were able to tread water through 2020 and into 2021, which is where we find ourselves today.

Let's share wisdom!

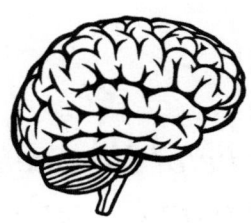

"Never overlook where the person you know today will be in years to come so make the effort to always keep in touch."

Liz Brewer
Party planner to the stars

"Ask for help! No-one can do it on their own and together everyone achieves more."

Sally Marshall
Publisher & author

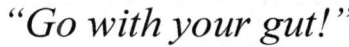

"Go with your gut!"

Paul Hargreaves
Entrepreneur & author 'Forces for Good'

"Personal networking is not "paper trust"; it is relationship trust. It's the result of someone trusting you enough to refer you with the belief that the engagement is infinite."

Robert Jones
Founder & Chairman iNETpreneur Network
Best-selling author, speaker & radio show host

"The riches are in the niches."

Frank King
Comedian

"Learn to sell - don't delegate this initially. Only start recruiting sales people once you have a proven sales process. To sell you have to really understand the customer's problem so focus on that. Listen and playback the challenges faced then focus on solving them."

Hatty Fawcett
FOCUSED for business

"Know your trade very well, and stay focussed."

Priya Mishr
CEO, board member & author

"Did you know most of the start-ups in the U.S. are launched by people aged 45 and older? Start Small. Start Smart. Start Right Now."

Rick Terrien
Author & board member - Center for ageless entrepreneurs

"Don't try to change other's view try to understand why they hold them."

Lord Mark Price
Founder WorkL
Chairman Fairtrade foundation
Minister of State trade and investment
Former MD Waitrose

"Let the manager manage."

John Treharne
Founder - The Gym Group

"As any business owner knows, it is difficult to turn over responsibilities to someone else. When you find dedicated and capable individuals, encourage them to shine. Make them a part of the team and allow them to contribute to the future vision of the company. Hard work, along with these solid employees, will be the key to your success."

Kim Strabley
Trade exchange owner

"Don't get distressed if people you wish to engage with don't respond at first. It's easy to think they don't want to respond but in many cases they are just too busy and your issue isn't a priority for them. So, persist in chasing/ following up until you get a definite No!"

Ivor Tucker
Corporate trade exchange & SCR expert

"Risk winning every day in response to the guaranteed uncertainty that is our entrepreneurial world."

Dr Jacqui Taylor
Cyberpreneur Top 20 UK entrepreneur / UN Advisor / G20 Advisor

"Sad, happy or somewhere in between – keep posting!"

Ed Zia
International Master Coach & Marketing Mentor FAMI CPM

"Know your numbers."

Dr Richard Strongman
Managing Director - Harvest Fine Foods

"If you do today, what you did yesterday, you cannot expect a different result tomorrow. Therefore plan your way to a successful future."

James Short CB OBE
Major General British Army [retired]

"Without challenge there is no achievement. It has stood me is good stead throughout my career and is very much based on complex problem solving, resilience, overcoming adversity and working hard"

Jon Dutton
CEO Rugby League World Cup 2021

Business Blunders and Bloody Great Ideas

Johnisms

Johnism 16

Make it easy as possible for a customer to buy from you. I went to get a new car and the salespeople had to get some facts and figures from me. I had to jump through all sorts of hoops before we got to the good stuff. I had to get identification. I sent them over my debit card. No good. It didn't match the criteria. I sent them my driving licence. I sent them my passport. Bingo! That matched their criteria. Fantastic! Then they wanted an electricity bill. Why? I'm not sure I know the answer, but to get a new car I had to provide an electricity bill to the people that were supposed to be selling the car to me. The lesson here is, don't make it difficult for the customer to buy from you. Take a good look at your business and try to understand the pain point where your systems and processes are getting in the way. Are you putting up barriers and hurdles that actually stop people buying from you?

Nugget tip – Ask customers for feedback on their buying experience with you.

Johnism 17

Never discount, always add value. Businesses that discount only degrade their product and attract bad customers because people that only buy from you on price will only buy from you when you've got a cheap price. And it gets worse. Not only do they only buy from you when it's a cheap price, they tell their friends, and birds of a feather flock together so all you get is all the cheapskates doing business with you. What's more, they're the ones that are going to cause you 80% of your problems. They are the moaners who going to be saying: 'You didn't do this. You didn't do that.' Businesses that appreciate the value in your goods and services are good customers. So never discount, always add value.

Johnism 18

All buyers are liars. If you're a sales person out in the marketplace you have to recognise that all buyers are liars! It's true! And all of us are buyers so we're all liars! I don't care who you are, but we all tell lies when we go to buy. Have you ever been into a shop and the assistant comes up and says: 'Hello. Can I help you?' You say: 'No thanks, I'm just looking.'? If that was true, then why did you walk into the shop in the first place? Was it raining outside? I doubt it. You went in there with a purpose in mind. What probably happened is that the shop assistant asked a bad question, but even so you still told a lie in response to it. All buyers are liars.

Pivotal Moment

I love my cricket. When I owned the car rental business every Sunday we'd take a half-day off. It was my release. Every business owner needs their 'cricket'.

I was getting to the end of my playing career, getting old and grumpy. I was a left arm orthodox spin bowler. I always used to pitch it on middle stump and it'd go straight on rather than spin too much. One day I took exception to the batsman, I was continually appealing for leg before wicket and this umpire kept on saying that it was not out. This was back in the days prior to the DRS and all the other modern technologies that we've got today.

I lost my cool, told the umpire what I thought of him, and ended up – bizarrely enough – getting suspended. As part of my suspension, other than some weeks off, I had to undertake an umpiring course, which was an odd condition, but there it was.

So, I went along to this course and, lo and behold, I thought: 'This is all right.' I passed the test okay. I enjoyed it. So when I retired from playing I began umpiring at a very low level, third or fourth grade on the Gold Coast. In the first year, I umpired the semi-final of third grade in the final series. In my second year, I got promoted onto the first-grade list and ended up doing the first grade semi-final, which included my own former team, which was a very hard moment and not without controversy as people couldn't see how I would not be biased, which is another story. But I got through that okay.

Having moved to the UK, I went through all the ranks and ended up being in the top echelon of non-professional umpires in the world. Out of 9,000 umpires in the UK, I was in the top 20 or 30 and met some very interesting people. I've umpired on television, umpired the final of the Minor Counties four-day championship, umpired the final of the national knockout. It was a great time meeting some great people under some wonderful circumstances.

Obviously, the point of the story is without being suspended I might never have discovered umpiring. Maybe that situation occurred to push me onto another path. I'm glad it did.

Chapter 7
Seek out solutions

During the pandemic we spent a lot of time trying to understand the state of play. We needed to know where we were at in order to make good decisions about how we moved forwards. In 2020 we observed that globally BBX had lost approximately 30,000 clients during Covid – a massive hit for any business to take and we heard a lot of people moaning and complaining and whingeing and blaming the government for this and the government for doing that.

That was when we decided to put on the Quantum Leap Business Show to try and get 40 or 50 or 60 of my strongest contacts that owned businesses and were thought leaders to join in the world's first 24 hour non-stop global event for action and opportunity – a mix of business and personal inspiration to get us thinking and working out the way forward. It is the reason why a windscreen is 40 times bigger then a rear vision mirror !

We staged the first show back in December 2020 and within two months, we'd gathered around 50 thought leaders from all over the world. We had people like Kevin Byrne, who started Checkatrade.com out of his garage in 1998 and sold it 20 years later for £78 million; Allan Pease, who I'd known back in the 1970s in my insurance days – he's sold 30 million books around the world on body language; and Jeff Fenech, the Australian world boxing champion in three weight divisions, who was a BBX ambassador.

We asked all of them questions about how they dealt with adversity. The idea was to give some Nugget tips, inspiration and ideas to the business owners that were still stuck like the rabbit in the headlights due to Covid.

Jeff Fenech came up with a great one. He reminded me that at one time he had trained Mike Tyson so he knows better than anyone that everybody's got a plan until you get a smack in the face.

The parallels with Covid are plain to see. You might have a plan, the best plan ever, but when Covid comes along that plan means nothing. We have no control over Covid. Nobody saw it coming. Nobody forecast it. Nobody could have ever imagined what it would be like, but then... Bang! Smack! It's on you.

But it's how you react that is the important part.

It's that Nugget again: Expect the unexpected!

So when a crisis does happen you need to take swift, decisive action, which is what we did. You can't be stuck going: 'Oh, me. Oh, my.' And, to be truthful, I don't care which side of politics you're on, but Boris Johnson and the team in the UK Government at the time, which were faced with the biggest crisis since the war, dealt with it magnificently in my opinion. It also highlighted the response by in particular Sir Keir Starmer – always criticizing never providing solutions ! I say to any of my team – " Lets review where did we do well and how can we improve " Any idiot can criticize but it takes a leader and a thinker to initiate a solution !

Certainly, when compared to some of the countries that BBX operates in – like Thailand where the Government gave no assistance whatsoever. If I hear anybody here in the UK moaning, I just refer them to Thailand – go and talk to a Thai business owner and see how he's or she's getting on at the moment.

The Quantum Show was planned for 23 December, two days before Christmas. The general feeling was that we can't put a show on two days before Christmas, people will only be thinking about Christmas, but my sense was everyone is stuck in their homes, they won't be out shopping so let's put a show on. That was exactly what we did and we ended up getting 37,800 unique impressions to this first virtual event.

Previously, when we had a live BBX event, people had to travel to a certain venue and you'd hear from people saying they couldn't get there as it was more than an hour away, or it was a Sunday and no good for them. So we did with this event online and put it on for 24 hours, starting here in the UK then moving around the world. We had interviews, workshops, virtual networking events, anything that would generate ideas, inspiration, and tips for the people that were watching. Afterwards, we had a six-week exhibition all online.

For a first event it was great, but it didn't do everything. It didn't look like turning up at the ExCel Centre in London and walking into the lobby and feeling as though you were at a show. We decided that we needed to build our own software to run the show as we wanted. That was the experience we wanted for our customers.

By reaching out to one of our franchise partners who's got strong connections in India, we ended up building the platform that we wanted. Now the show is like walking into an auditorium. You've got the information booth, then you can go off to the exhibition centre, or the theatre playing with the next instalment of the show from a thought leader that's dropping gold Nuggets like they were going out of fashion!

In other areas you can just sit and have a one-to-one with somebody. Your network is your net worth.

I'm sure it's true for many other people as well but one of the benefits of Covid is that it has given us the opportunity to take stock – some precious time to think and plan how you can structure your business going forward. Of course, much of that will be online, over and above what we're already doing, it's going to increase our international trading.

One of the early goals for BBX was to trade with other countries, but the practicality was that most of people prefer to trade in their own home country so even though you could build a website in India and have it delivered to Australia, people were reluctant to move into that space. Covid though has accelerated online opportunities. We've just restructured our entire platform and are also in the process of rolling out AI with the development of an incredible new app.

I think the other thing is remote working. Since the first lockdown lots of people have got used to working from home, but it's not for everyone and you need to bring them back into the office environment. For me, I don't think remote working is a forever strategy, at least not exclusively. I think if you've got remote workers, where possible you need to get them back into the office, even if it's one week a month.

The entire team at BBX will continue to meet every six months or so. We get everybody together in one group, go away for a weekend somewhere and deliver some training as well as fun. For me that's how to motivate and inspire the team.

The other area we are developing is crypto currency collaboration – a currency of the future, as opposed to the digital trade credits that BBX was founded on. Blockchain is here to stay and I believe we will gradually see an increase in Blockchain reliance on just about everything we're dealing with, from medical records to property ownership and shares and all sorts of things, it will all be on a Blockchain.

In fact, and here's a Nugget for you. I think that the whole world of currency, as we know it, will disappear within my lifetime. Now that's what I call a Nugget prediction.

Seek out solutions

Let's share wisdom!

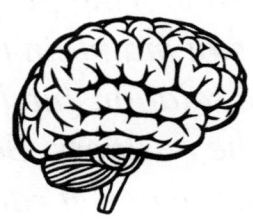

"The first profit is always the best profit and always leave something in it for someone else."

David Harding
Chartered Surveyor

"The forces that bring people together in business do not maintain the partnership long term. The relationship has to evolve and mature with the business. Be prepared to go it alone from the outset rather than select a partner who seems on the same page but ultimately is not. The old adage 'the ship most likely to sink is a partnership' might sound cliché but is completely true."

David Cliff
Business mentor of the year

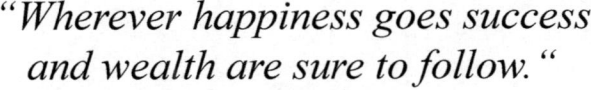

"Wherever happiness goes success and wealth are sure to follow."

Croz Crossley
The Mindset Master

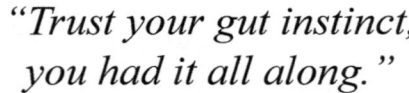

"Trust your gut instinct, you had it all along."

Mary Pagano
NED Entrepreneur

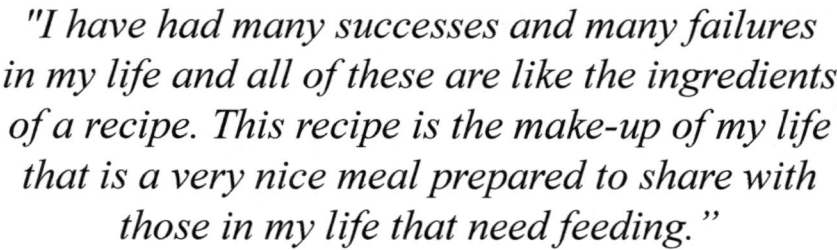

"I have had many successes and many failures in my life and all of these are like the ingredients of a recipe. This recipe is the make-up of my life that is a very nice meal prepared to share with those in my life that need feeding."

David Brock
Founder - Your Partnerships

"Be passionate about what you do - it's contagious."

Kath Pay
CEO, author & keynote speaker

"You need a clear VISION of where you want the business to be in five years. It must be written down on paper and form the basis for your business plan with forecasts for five years, twelve months, and one month. All your subsequent business decisions will stem from asking yourself, does this fit with my business?"

Geoff Head
Founder – Protel

"Do one thing that pushes you forward every single day. This will help you to grow faster than anything else. Have a plan, stick to the plan, and if the plan fails there is always plan B."

Maddy Alexander Grout
Founder - My VIP card and Crowd funding success

"Share knowledge and insights in a clear, simple, and understandable style."

Lance Scouler
The savvy navigator & Amazon Influencer

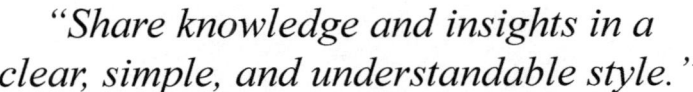

"Keep your eyes on the road ahead – success and failure are hidden just around the corner. But that's why you chose the driving seat!"

Les Abbott – Fryer
Owner - Dayfold

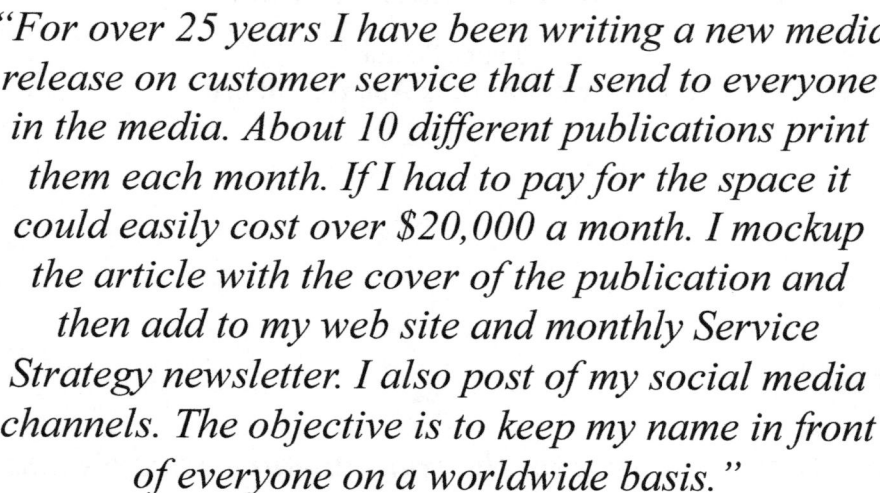

"For over 25 years I have been writing a new media release on customer service that I send to everyone in the media. About 10 different publications print them each month. If I had to pay for the space it could easily cost over $20,000 a month. I mockup the article with the cover of the publication and then add to my web site and monthly Service Strategy newsletter. I also post of my social media channels. The objective is to keep my name in front of everyone on a worldwide basis."

John Tschohl
President Service Quality Institute for 50 years

"Most brands take years to build. Founders could do far worse than to implement the Japanese philosophy of Kaizen. That is, to aim to make small and regular improvements to their business over a long period of time, and not giant and immediate leaps. Business should be treated as a long game, and it's one that demands patience. It can take 10 years to truly establish oneself, even in a local market."

Josh Simons
Hospitality entrepreneur

"Life skills are sales skills! and there's no such word as can't."

Jules White
Speaker, author & Clubhouse moderator

"Starting my day with a clear head & heart is essential. Meditation is my morning ritual giving me the clarity to align my values with my purpose each day: this without a doubt is the most important thing I could share with future business leaders and entrepreneurs."

Jarvis Smith
Co Founder - My Green Pod.com and Founder - P.E.A awards

" E+M=S
That's Entrepreneurship, + Management = Success.
Entrepreneurs, generally, make for naff managers, they're too busy thinking up the next big thing. Managers, generally, make for naff entrepreneurs, they're too busy implementing the systems and processes to make the next big thing possible. So put the two together, and that is the winning equation."

James Sinclair
CEO - Partyman

"In business as in life - never take someone's choice away from them. They must live with the consequences of their decisions."

John Shenton
Personality profiler

A Nugget I learned from my wife.

Part of my success in the last 20 years is due to my wife. Linda is my calming influence, my rock. She is the calming influence of sensibility.

She'll ask: 'Are you really sure that you want to do this? What about that? What about this?' While she's never negative, she's very intelligent and always brings the woman's intuition and I don't know if that's a general thing, but she's certainly got it. She's got such a great feel and a great eye for character.

Many of the business deals I've done over the years, she's met the person that I've been talking to, and she'll have a quiet word and say: 'John, I don't like that person. I don't trust them'; or 'John, I like that person' and, and I'll tell you what, 99 times out of a hundred she's spot on.

So the nugget I've learned is to make sure you get a partner who compliments what you do rather than simply serves you – someone that you can talk to like that is a great asset, both in your business and in your life. Thanks, Linda!

Business Blunders and Bloody Great Ideas

Johnisms

Johnism 19

Kick out the jams! Get rid of the people who jam up your life. It doesn't matter if it's in in business or in your personal life, block and delete all the toxic people. As soon as you encounter one, and you'll know immediately who they are, freeze them out. If they post a negative comment on your LinkedIn post, or if they have a go at you directly, or goad you by saying something that's in direct contravention to your principles and beliefs, ignore them. Don't rise to the bait. Don't give them the satisfaction of a response. That just gives them oxygen. Just hit the block button. Hit delete. Remove the post. Make sure you never talk to them again. When you block and delete toxic people, what you are left with are good people, and good people are the ones you want to be surrounded by, for your business and for your mental health.

Johnism 20

There are three types people in this world – those who make things happen, those who watch things happen, and those who ponder what the hell just happened. Be one of the people who make things happen. I picked up a saying from a colleague many, many years ago, and it has stood by me all my life. It says: 'Don't run upstairs. Don't back odds on, and look after your mother.' I love my mother. For those of you who like a punt here and there, I used to run racehorses and when they got to odds on, they were always a bad bet. So never back odds on. And anybody who's ever tried to run upstairs, you trip over and you fall on your arse, and that's not a good thing. So, be told, don't run upstairs, don't back odds on, and look after your mother!

Johnism 21

Tackling big changes is like eating an elephant. Right, before anybody from an animal protection society gets carried, that is a metaphor, so don't get tight, people. My point is that tackling big challenges is like eating an elephant. It's a big job. You need to size it up and develop a strategy, but ultimately you can only eat it one chunk at a time. That's a great thing. Brian Tracy, a long-time friend of mine that most people will have heard of, wrote a book entitled Eat That Frog!: 21 Great Ways to Stop Procrastinating and Get More Done in Less Time. His point was we need to chunk away at the stuff that gets the hardest to digest, but do it one chunk at a time.

Johnism 22

Outsource everything you don't like or you're not good at. I see people all the time in business and they spend hours doing their books, or doing their website – tasks they are absolutely hopeless at. All they end up with our bad outcomes. What's more, they end up having a bad life because they're not enjoying what they're doing. Instead, focus on the stuff that you like and are good at, get rid of and outsource all the stuff you don't like and not good at to people that do like and are good at it. That's a mantra that I've always lived by.

And then, finally, people will ask: 'A lot of these things are great, John. How do you do all these things? Where do you find all the money from?' And I'd hark back to the spare capacity opportunity in your business. Capture and monetise spare capacity and use it to fund some of the things that I've just spoken about.

John's case studies & Random thoughts

Case Study One

It was a Sunday. I was out driving with my wife and two adult children in our hometown of Bournemouth and I came across a sign at the side of the road that said: 'New Pizza Oven Under New Management Come and Try'.

I turned up the driveway lined with trees and when I got to the top, there it was, The Pear At Parley. I went to the door and was greeted well by the person at reception who invited us to have a drink beforehand or we could go outside. It was a lovely sunny day, so I said: 'I'll go outside and see the new pizza oven.' The grounds of the restaurant had far-reaching views of Bournemouth; it was a beautiful place for lunch.

We ordered our pizza, started lunch, and then just as we're about to have our first mouthfuls the waitress asks: 'How's your pizza?' and you think: 'Go away, I don't want to do that right now. I'm just about to take my first bite.'

Of course, you politely you say: 'Yes, it's all okay, thanks very much.'

But just a tip here, a little Nugget – if you are running a restaurant train your staff to give diners the breathing space to at least get into a meal.

Anyway, we finished the meal, paid the bill, and we're walking out the door, and I said to my wife: 'Wow, these guys missed one of the biggest opportunities ever.'

They failed to capture any of our data – no name, no address, no email or phone contact. Nothing. They had no idea about us at all. They could have asked for a point of contact and asked the month of my birth. Who could object to that? If they had got that, they could have then contacted me a month before I was going to have my birthday and said: 'Hey, would you like to come back and eat at the restaurant? You know, bring a friend and we'll give you a little birthday present. Our treat.'

They had no data capture and to this day, they still have no clue who we are.

This was a couple of years ago and, of course, because of that they had no way of inviting me back. There was never an invitation to return. And to this day I've never been back.

They should have asked me why I'd turned into their driveway in the first place, what was my motivation for visiting?

But all they asked me was: 'Did you like the meal?' And here in the UK, people are polite. They just say: 'Yeah, it was nice.' Even if they didn't like it they'd rather say they did and then just don't bother going back again. In Australia or America or other places, they throw a rock at you if it wasn't any good and you know it straight away, but here you've got to be a little bit more subtle.

Two years later, I still haven't been back to that place. They still haven't written to me. They still haven't given me an offer and they won't invite me to return. They still haven't got a clue what made me go in for that day.

In fact, it was the little sign about the new pizza oven. Now, if I was in the marketing department and I had that information I'd be able to make a bigger sign or put it in more places or whatever it happens to be. These are simple ideas, but so many businesses miss these opportunities. I call this surviving despite your best efforts not to.

I speak around the world on this subject: why 50% of people in business survive despite their best efforts not to and the others fail. So don't be one of the ones who fails.

Case Study Two

Don't remove your flower boxes!

I worked with a group of Indian restaurants that had pretty little flower boxes outside their doors. I was talking to the owner, and this was back during the global financial crisis of 2008, and they were working on better ways of getting more people into the group of restaurants.

The owner was talking about taking away all the flower boxes and turning them into outside eating areas.

In the UK that's fine for three months in summer, but the weather doesn't really allow outdoor eating as well as it does in other parts of the world. So I asked him: 'Have you surveyed customers to find out what the buying motivation is for them to come into the restaurant?'

Like too many other restaurant owners his response was: 'No.'

I suggested a 90-day survey to find out why people came into the restaurant. What was their buying motivation? What triggered their decision to come in through the door?

The findings were really interesting – 28% of the respondents, mostly women, said they loved the pretty flower boxes.

So, it wasn't the food and it wasn't the service and it wasn't anything else that the owner thought it might've been, it was the flower boxes!

So there you have it. If they had taken away the flower boxes they would have had a 28% dip in turnover and blamed it on the weather or some other thing that had nothing to do with the actual reason.

Case Study Three

We have an excellent charity that I work with in Bournemouth called Diverse Abilities. It helps people with learning difficulties, from young people right up to octogenarians.

A few years ago the charity staged a fundraising ball at Lighthouse, Poole's Centre for the Arts and rang me a week before to say they had five tables that hadn't sold. Five tables of 10 people worth a £1,000 a table left them with a significant hole in their budget. They had of course paid all the infrastructure costs, paid for the venue, paid for the catering and had a five grand hole to fill.

I got together with my account management team and we secured five companies for them that bought the tables using their BBX credits. So, Diverse Abilities earned £5,000 by using digital trade credits through BBX.

I then connected them with Paul Sandy, one of our jewellery customers on BBX and the charity bought a diamond ring worth £5,000 using the BBX credits they had earned from the sale of the tables. The ring was raffled on the night and raised £12,500.

And that's how a charity that would've had a £5,000 hole in the floor but turned it into £12,500 in revenue simply by using BBX to convert spare capacity into held value to add value to their event rather than leave a hole.

You can see why I love BBX!

AND ANOTHER THING...

Queues annoy me so much!

I first arrived in the UK in 2003. On my first day I was at Richmond-on-Thames, a lovely place. I was walking down the street at lunchtime and there was a queue snaking out of doorway. Curiosity got the better of me so I walked up to the guy at the end of the queue and asked: 'What's going on here, mate?' He replied: 'It's McDonalds. It's lunchtime.'

I just shook my head. They had five people on the tills and one large queue of people feeding into these five points of sale. People were bored and goofing off in the queue and not paying attention, and that was creating the extra wait. If they just got people to fall into five queues, they would have dealt with the volume of hungry people a lot quicker.

I don't know why it's a very British thing to queue. It's just bizarre. But my point with the McDonald's story is this: Don't allow people to form queues in your business, make sure you deal with them promptly.

How many times have you rung your bank or the utility company and the phone rings forever? Then you hear that annoying voice: 'At this time we're experiencing far greater call demand than usual'; or 'All our operators are busy. Have you tried our website?'

Have you tried our website? Have I tried your website? What they're trying to do is play with your brain and get you off the call and onto their website. What about the people who like talking to a human being? You've got a problem and you want to talk to a human, not a chat bot or an online facility.

How many times have I found myself with a question and found myself online directed to FAQs, frequently asked questions? Did this help? No! I just want to talk to somebody.

The reason bigger companies are trying to cut down their call centre staff and blaming COVID, which really gets up my nose because it's not COVID at all, is because they're trying to decrease their staff overheads and put everything online. And people are not robots.

So, don't let your customers form a queue to get into your business.

Rant over!

AND ONE MORE THING...

What to do when it's not working.

I have a couple of Nuggets here on what to do when things aren't going the way you'd like them to. We've all been there and there is always a solution if you look for it.

1. If it ain't broke don't fix it, but if it's not working, change it. An oldie; but a goldie. It means that if you continue to do what you've always done, you will not get what you've always got before. Once upon a time you would, but in this modern age we've moved the six degrees of separation down to probably about 1.8, in my opinion.

Largely because of modern ways of connecting, I believe.

So, if it's not working reach out to someone who might be able to help solve your problem. That way you get expertise that's outside your field and if you ask for help in a genuine way in my experience most people say yes.

2. Refocus on the important things. Out of a hundred tasks, 20 of those tasks drive 80% of your outcomes. As I mentioned earlier, I'd urge everybody to read The 80/20 Principle: The Secret of Achieving More with Less by Richard Koch. He advises we focus in on the 20 activities that are driving 80% of our

outcomes. Taken to its logical conclusion it could even mean, get rid of the 80% of customers that are only providing 20% of your revenue.

3. Commit to the 'yes'. We've never experienced fear and uncertainty like with we did with COVID. They have been very uncertain times and many businesses ended up in paralysis. The definition of paralysis is getting stuck in an environment where you go round and round in ever decreasing circles until you finally disappear up your own backside! When people are in fear, they end up in paralysis, which leads to inaction and inaction is a killer. So I would say to anybody that's fearful, the biggest fear that faces you looks in the mirror every morning is fear itself. It's the fear of the unknown. Take a risk, take a gamble and ask yourself a question before you take an action. What's the worst that can happen? And if the worst that can happen is not death, then do it. Say yes, and then work out how to do it later. But get committed to the 'yes'.

4. Keep the end in mind. Keep the end in mind and then work out the details. Like Brian Tracy said with sales focus, you have a beginning and you have an end. Focus on the end and work your way backwards. The side conversation is how you're going to do it. Work out where you want to go first, and then work out the detail later. It's like going on holidays. People put more planning into going on holidays than they do running their business. Now, when you go on holiday, first you decide where you're going then you have a look and see where the hotels and the restaurants are, what attractions there are, how you are going to get there and where's the limo going to be. But you have to start with the destination before you can do all the intricate planning. Have a nice holiday!

Case Study Four - The Cat Café

We had an instance a few years ago where a lovely lady who used to work for one of our charities came to me and said: 'John, I want to set up a cat café.'

My response was: 'What's a cat café?' And she said: 'Well cats are therapeutic. People would come to the cat café and have a cup of coffee and a biscuit and they get to stroke the cats that are running around.'

I thought it was the craziest idea I'd ever heard. Interesting, but crazy.

Anyway, she was determined to do it, but in order to open she needed to raise money to pay for all the usual setup costs facing a new business like fit out signs design furniture etc.

I liked her so I agreed to help create a plan. We came up with a scheme to pay suppliers with a 'future voucher' in the business. Someone would provide £20 in work value and they'd get a £40 voucher to spend at the cat café in the future, or use as they wanted to. So to the suppliers by doing it when they had otherwise downtime it was like getting double price ! They could use the vouchers themselves or perhaps as a gift or also sell them to me to turn into BBX money that they could use to pay an accountant or do some advertising or even get their vans serviced!

When people came in to redeem the vouchers, her only costs were the coffee and cake, so to provide a £40 voucher might only cost her six or eight pounds for the actual ingredient because none of the fixed cost like rent or wages changed! It also saved her cash upfront when she only sending money and not earning any!

It attracted new customers into the café. And of course, a busy café always attracts interest and yet more customers.

Case Study Five - AFC Bournemouth

AFC Bournemouth are an English football team. They were in the Premier League and might again be soon, but for now are in the second tier, the Championship.

However, at the time of this story, AFC Bournemouth were in League Two, the fourth tier of English football and the lowest level of the professional English Football League. I had meeting with Rob, the Commercial Manager, and walking into the stadium for the first time the signage around the ground caught my eye. Rob told me that most of the space around the pitch level was sold, but as I looked across the pitch I saw a big open space about 90 metres wide and three or four metres high. It was behind the seats on the far grandstand, which was opposite where the directors and most of the crowd usually sat. At that time, the stadium capacity was about 10,000, but the average crowd was three or four thousand.

I said to Rob: 'How come you haven't sold that space?' He said: 'Well, It's not TV facing.' To which I replied: 'How many home games do you have a year?' He told me it was about thirty, but only one or two were televised.

I had to recap. They didn't sell advertising on that section of the ground because it didn't get shown on TV, but they only had a couple of games a year on TV and what about the 5,000 people that sit in the stand facing it? They would obviously see the advertising boards from their sitting position and many of them went to all (or nearly all) the home games.

In the end, my company sponsored that space, paying for it in digital trade credits. We turned it into the biggest ad sign in the Football League, 90 metres wide, and three metres high. And there it sat. After a couple of seasons when my contract finished, they then sold that for hard cash bringing new revenue into the football club at a time when it was starting to climb its way up the leagues. Hopefully next season they will be back in the premier league and that sign will be worth £60 - £100 thousand a year [ok so a months wages for a player these days but that's another story!]

So the advertising worked and I attracted over a 100 new customers over 3 years and the club used the digital trade credits to offset cash costs like security accommodation for loan players from London printing etc at a time when they were within hours of folding!

That was a fantastic case study of taking spare capacity and turning it into value simply by keeping our eyes and ears open and looking for opportunity. It's all about awareness! What do you have in your business that you could turn into revenue right now?

Case Study Six - Dealing with Crisis

When COVID struck in the early part of 2020 one of my clients was a Bulgarian sock manufacturer. Their socks were very high quality, with reinforced heels and toes. Pre-COVID they had a turnover of around $1.7 million, but when the pandemic struck, production ceased and the obvious thought was: 'What are we going to do now?'

The answer turned out to be really simple – they turned their sock manufacturing plant into a factory making masks!

It turns out the manufacturing process elements are actually very similar so all they had to do was stop making socks and start making masks, rejigging the machinery. As a direct result, they ended up increasing their turnover in about eight months from $1.7 million to nearly $8 million. It was the same factory, the same staff, the same processes, but retooled and rejigged machinery. They leveraged four times what they were getting before, during one of the worst periods in economic world history.

I think this is a fantastic example of creativity in action.

It reminded me of a similar instance back in Australia in the late 1990s. My client Tom Tate, who's a longstanding friend, owned a hotel and was very reliant on the in-bound Asian tourist market. The hotel was occupied pretty much 90% of the time by large tour groups coming in from various parts of Asia.

When the Asian financial crisis hit in 1997, [there seems to be a re-occurring theme here with world events over which the small business owner cannot see coming and has no control over] he went from nearly 100% occupancy to almost zero. In the space of a week or two. So, a little bit like COVID, this was a bus hitting him head on.

Tom and I got together and we came up with a strategy involving leverage and spare capacity. We worked out that average tour operator rate that he was getting for a room that could take up to four people was $60 for the night. That was the rate that he had to give the tourist operator in order to get their business. So it wasn't their normal prevailing rate, but it was the cut rate in order to get bulk business.

When these bulk bookings suddenly dried up, the thought was how to replace the lost income. Tom still had all the staff, he had all the overheads, but very little revenue coming in.

So, to attract new customers we came up with the idea of selling vouchers that could be exchanged in the hotel bar. The vouchers were valued at $20 each and you could get four drinks. For every room night the customer had to buy 4 @ $20 bar vouchers so if the room had 4 friends had to drink 4 drinks each night so a no brainer!

In addition to that, they also got PAID a dollar for each person for each night. So the promotion was "We'll pay YOU a $1 a night to come and stay all you have to do is buy four drinks at the bar!"

The cost of providing four drinks was maybe $4 for the alchohol and by paying someone a dollar to come and stay in your property was another dollar so $5 cost per person per night . So you were starting off at about $80 for the room from voucher sales , but after costs, you got back down to the same $60 that you had before from the tourist operator ! If the people forgot to use all of their vouchers even more ! In fact the average breakage or non-redeemed rate for vouchers globally is 28%.

At this time Tom was also the President of the Surfers Paradise Chamber of Commerce. He devised a PR campaign showing that a tour operator has to pay to get people to come into his hotel, and that was the headline. There he was front page of the local Gold Coast Bulletin pockets turned out with great big headline " Chamber President PAYING $1 a night for guests to stay in his hotel ".

Of course, the media picked it up and the next thing we knew, he was on Channel Four, one of Australia's national television channels. They had the general manager of the local Marriott Hotel come on the show and say that the Chamber's President was bastardising the industry, and it was a terrible thing for the Gold Coast region to have someone paying people to come and stay in their hotel. How was he ever going to service this? It was the most ridiculous thing that they ever heard of and he'd go broke tomorrow.

Tom got huge publicity out of the situation and, bear in mind he was still getting the $60 a night at the hotel, it was one of the best ways of using spare capacity and leverage that I've ever come across.

John's case studies & random thoughts

Case Study Seven – Unsold capacity

How to win cash contracts by using the unsold capacity that you have in your business.

For the purpose of this exercise, I'll use a legal firm as an example. Let's say that the legal firm can be either a sole trader or it could have a few partners within it, and it wants a new piece of business.

It pitches that business to a potential customer – let's say that customer grows vegetables. For whatever reason, they haven't been able to get the contract across the line – this happens quite often, let's say the contract is worth £10,000 pounds and vegetable grower wants to do the deal but doesn't have the money.

Now, if the legal firm has got spare capacity, without increasing overhead an opportunity to leverage that spare capacity exists.

It could go to the vegetable grower and say: 'As an introduction to our firm, we'll accept £10,000 of vegetables for our legal services.'

If the vegetable grower agrees, and they have that spare capacity, then everyone is happy.

The only issue now is, what does the legal firm do with £10,000 of vegetables?

They could give or sell the vegetables to charity or distribute the veg to staff, but if the legal firm was a BBX customer they could sell the vegetables to the BBX community. That way, they have £10,000 in BBX money and be able to do the legal work for the farmer because they have been paid. The farmer has then paid their legal bill with produce they may not have sold and if the end users like the vegetables they could return and so the farmer has picked up new customers as a result of paying a bill!

If the legal firm do good work with that new client, it's a toe in the water, they've maintained their price, and they've got £10,000 with BBX to offset the cash cost in their business. Crucially though, they've won a new client and when the term renews, the vegetable grower will feel compelled to use the same law firm because they like them and will pay them in pounds Sterling going forward.

That's what I call winning cash contracts. And that can apply to just about any business that's looking to pick up new business.

Case Study Eight - Property

I'm going to finish with a story about property because it's a great way of investing otherwise worthless unsold spare capacity.

A property developer I was working with came to me and told me he had a thirty-two unit development in a cul-de-sac. His initial forecasts valued the properties at an average price of $220,000 each with the two closest to the busy road at the top of the cul-de-sac at $179,000 and the dearest at the end of it at $ 249,000 . This gave a project finished value of $7,040,000 to which he had bank finance approval . He had bought the site for $950,000 and had obtained planning subsequently and so after taking away the estimated cost to construct of $156,200 for each one stood to make around $800,000 profit.

He approached me and asked if he could sell 10 of these with 20% deposits using trade credits because he figured he could spend the $440,000 he would get on construction costs from suppliers in my community which seemed reasonable . He could also spend any unspent amount on a new project so we both happy.

Then I had a thought!

What would the numbers look like if we sold the two hardest to sell at the beginning of the cul-de-sac FIRST on FULL digital trade credit but at $199,000?

It would establish a price and if those sold for that amount why wouldn't the remainder sell at an increased price based on those sales?

He put that through the number crunching machine and bingo! It would lift the total sale price for the project by $640,000!

We sold the two in the first day of the opening sale for full trade credits to two well pleased customers , created a market for the rest of the development, created a price for the rest of the development, and at the end of the development, they ended up selling the thirty other ones for a total of $550,000 more than what they had originally estimated!

So, they'd not only earned $550,000 extra CASH yield in the property or a massive 68% INCREASE in pre tax profits, but it also earned $398,000 trade to then offset some of the cash costs in developing the property, the marketing, and so forth.

That's a great example of setting a price and using spare capacity to your advantage.

My Nuggets on recruitment
John's Recruitment Tips

Recruitment is a big topic now because a lot of firms that I've come across are having trouble with it. They rely on the expensive way of recruiting that you have no control over – putting an ad online or in a paper. You pay for the ads then cross your fingers because you have no control over the responses either in quantity or quality.

The other common method is to use a recruitment company. At least you have a degree of control over the cost because you should be able to negotiate a deal where you pay an agreed percentage of the first year salary of the recruit and get a free replacement if that person once contracted leaves within an agreed period – commonly 90 days. The only issue you then have is that someone on say a £30,000 salary will cost between £3,000 and £6,000! Some recruiters offer a set monthly contract, but unless you are recruiting a certain number of people every month it too becomes a regular expense irrespective of outcome!

Here are a few Nuggets that I use with recruitment in general that allow you to have total control over outcome and in addition will not cost you much, if anything, to fund.

1. Recruit when you don't need to and you'll never be running around in panic mode. Many people that recruit only recruit once a vacancy occurs and then all of a sudden you're in shock mode because you have to start again. You've got a gap because there are persons leaving or have already left.

2. Take time over recruitment, make sure you recruit the right person and fire quickly. People get it round the wrong way. They recruit in a hurry and then take forever to fire the person and it's only when they fire them they realise it should have been done six months ago.

3. Talk to your existing customers and ask them who they would like to look after their account with you – it costs little or nothing. You could also include a value add as an incentive – if your customers refer someone they know that starts you will give them additional [say, £500 worth] of services etc.

4. Tell your staff you are expanding and ask them who would they like on the team to work along side them! Offer them an incentive that does not cost you much – if they nominate a successful candidate you give them a half day off perhaps Now, that's far less expensive than a recruitment company or an advert.

5. Always be recruiting… and I mean ALWAYS! Constantly be on the look out for outstanding people that you encounter in all aspects of your life.

6. Create 'Who Do You Know?' lists. Write down people you know or are acquainted with from school, hobbies, former companies etc.

7. Use social media. I prefer LinkedIn. Do polls or straight up posts – be consistent and be relentless – even if you don't need someone right at this moment.

8. Try not to recruit in your own image. Clones are for clowns! You need a diverse range of people, particularly if you are expending your teams.

9. Do not tick boxes; recruit the BEST person. I see a lot around quotas for gender and equality – both fine to strive for, but not at the expense of finding the best person for you and your business.

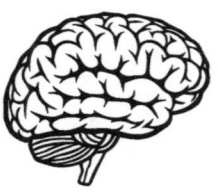

Gratitude

Thank you!

For those who have been associated with me in some way – big and small – all of you have contributed not only to my journey, but for all who follow, because as the human race evolves it must learn from the past to create a better future.

As the world shrinks with greater communication and connectivity [I believe the six degrees of separation is now probably two or three] the more you know the more you grow!

Individually, I must highlight the following people because they provided the pivotal moments so far in my life and business journey. Not always by design, However, the result so far would be radically different if I had never met you.

- Mum and Dad, for without their co-operation around October 1956 I would never have come into this world. [Oh, and why love is so important.]

- Mr Kaplan, my third form economics teacher, who taught me how to place bets on horse races to embellish my love for numbers and the economy.

- Tim Wadelton, my first business partner, creating a football pools scheme in third form that despite half the teachers being involved nearly got us expelled.

- The weedy guy at the dole office in Morwell whose advice to go on the dole made me think there was a better life than his miserable existence.

- Ren Forte, my first MLC manager, who was not the best sales manager but a great guy and the reason I got into sales.

- Brian Tracey, for his spine and ribs method of selling.

- Colin Grimshaw, my last MLC manager, who showed me what a really bad manager was and how a bad manager is the number one reason why someone leaves a company.

- Gerard Kerin, for introducing me to cricket.

- All the Goulburn Hawkes and Palm Beach Currumbin CC guys that taught me true friends need to be valued.

- David Johnstone, for being a great and trusted friend and business partner and to demonstrate why people like me need great follow up people in business.

- John Bunting, for introducing me to triangulation trading, and for showing how co-operation rather than competition leads to success.

- Gary Kamm, the ATO audit guy for attempting to drag me down to his level of public service mediocrity which made my mind up to never be anything other than a business owner.

- Wayne Sharpe, who showed me how to be ruthless with determination and drive.

- My current business partners Matt Harding and Scott Clancy for letting me be right. Ha!

- My wife Linda, for being my partner in life and the love of my life as well as the best sounding board and judge of character by pure instinct.

And lastly, thank you to you for reading. I hope you've found some Nuggets of wisdom and insights that resonate with you, and will perhaps in some way change the direction of your journey for the better.

What is your One Golden Nugget?
www.onegoldennugget.com